CARLA BLEY

AMERICAN

Composers

A list of books in the series appears
at the end of this book.

Carla Bley

Amy C. Beal

UNIVERSITY OF ILLINOIS PRESS

Urbana, Chicago, and Springfield

Library of Congress Cataloging-in-Publication Data
Beal, Amy C.
Carla Bley / Amy C. Beal.
p. cm.—(American composers)
Includes bibliographical references and index.
ISBN 978-0-252-03636-1 (cloth)—
ISBN 978-0-252-07818-7 (pbk.)
1. Bley, Carla.
2. Composers—United States—Biography.
3. Jazz musicians—United States—Biography.
I. Title.
ML410.B643B43   2011
781.65092—dc22   2011004562
[B]

For Steve Swallow

CONTENTS

ACKNOWLEDGMENTS   ix

Introduction: "Like a Mockingbird"   1

1. *Walking Woman*: Oakland, New York, Los Angeles, New York   5

2. *Sing Me Softly of the Blues*: *Early Short Pieces* and
   Songs without Words   15

3. *Social Studies*: The Jazz Composers Guild
   and the Jazz Composers Orchestra   27

4. "Mad at Jazz": *A Genuine Tong Funeral*   34

5. *Escalator over the Hill*: Jazz Opera as Fusion   41

6. *Copyright Royalties*: New Music Distribution Service   51

7. *Big Band Theory*: The Carla Bley Band and Other Projects   57

8. *The Lone Arranger*: History and Hilarity   65

9. *End of Vienna*: Fancy Chamber Music   75

10. *Dreams So Real*: "Jazz Is Really Where My Heart Now Lies"   83

NOTES   91

SUGGESTED LISTENING   99

SOURCES   101

INDEX   105

ACKNOWLEDGMENTS

I wish to sincerely thank Carla Bley and Steve Swallow for their warm and generous support of this project, for taking so much time to talk with me at their beautiful home, and for providing me with much appreciated materials. I am also indebted to the following people for talking with me about their work with Bley: Gary Burton, Charlie Haden, George Lewis, Karen Mantler, Michael Mantler, Timothy Marquand, Roswell Rudd, "Blue" Gene Tyranny, and Gary Valente. Several friends and correspondents helped me in various scholarly and practical ways while I was writing this book, and I wish to thank them as well: Gordon Beeferman, Amy Benson, Ran Blake, Michael Byron, Eric Drott, Guy Ducornet, Daniel Goode, Jo Hayward-Haines, Ellie Hisama, Jim and Zona Hostetler, Douglas Kahn, Paul Machlis, Jeff Magee, Leo McFadden, Noah Meites, Myra Melford, Cameron Mozee-Baum, Kate Peoples, Benjamin Piekut, Larry Polansky, Douglas Repetto, Eric Richards, Suzanne Roodman, Gayle Sherwood, Jeffrey Taylor, Ma'ayan Tsadka, Kent Underwood, and all my students who have taken an interest in this project. I am especially grateful to Ralf Dietrich for introducing me to the wonderful world of Carla Bley's music in the first place.

Laurie Matheson at University of Illinois Press has provided support and sound advice from the moment I mentioned this idea, and the encouraging yet cautionary voices of the two anonymous readers of my proposal were ever in my mind while writing. The scholars Sherrie Tucker and George Lewis offered much appreciated commentary on the manuscript in the later stages. In addition, I am thankful for the help of Edward Berger and Annie Kuebler at the Institute of Jazz Studies at Rutgers University. The University of California at Santa Cruz provided a greatly appreciated faculty research grant. During my research sabbatical in the autumn of 2009, the Center for Jazz Studies and the Department of Music at Columbia University graciously sponsored a public colloquium that

Acknowledgments

gave me an opportunity to begin sharing my research on Bley with a wider audience. Finally, I wish to thank my colleague Eric Porter and the graduate students in his jazz historiography seminar, taught at the University of California at Santa Cruz, during the spring of 2009. I appreciated their willingness to let me eavesdrop on their conversations, and I wrote this book armed with their insights.

CARLA BLEY

"I went west over toward Willow," what a country locution; the place was getting to him, "and I was up this one hill and heard some music. I have an ear for music."

"Do you?"

"Yup. Heard someone pounding out some complex damn tangled chords on a piano and came downhill following the sound. There was this big modern angled house, slate, pale wood, high triangular windows. I circled it. The music was coming from the basement. Someone was working through a sequence of these really dense ten-fingered chords—one chord, another, then a third, didn't like it, tried it another way, then another, then back, thrash thrash thrash, really beating the shit out of the music. It took me awhile to recognize the style and figure out that it was Carla Bley."

"Did you meet her?" Iris asked him, and the Bear was pleased to hear what might have been a note of jealousy in the music of her voice.

"Not today, but I did meet her one time when I was a cub and Jones took me down to Birdland on a leash. She was a cigarette girl at the time. I don't know if she remembers me from then, but recently I heard through Jones she'd like me in her band. I had to say no, of course."

"Why didn't you go in and introduce yourself?"

"Today? Naw. I just listened to her thrashing these chords out and thought, hey, if it's this much work for her maybe it's okay it's hard for me sometimes. That's intelligent, right?"

"In a touching, rudimentary way," Iris said.

"How I was finally sure it was Carla Bley's house, there were long tufts of frizzy blond hair tied to the chickenwire all around the garden—"

"That's strange."

"I think it's supposed to keep the deer from eating her vegetables."

—Rafi Zabor, *The Bear Comes Home*

Introduction

"Like a Mockingbird"

IN RAFI ZABOR'S JAZZ-HISTORICAL novel *The Bear Comes Home*, a saxophone-playing talking bear moves to Shady, in the New York Catskills. The sudden presence of Carla Bley in this otherwise mostly fictional novel, and the explicit references to certain facts about her life history and persona—a job as a "cigarette girl" at Birdland; an isolated life in Willow, New York; frizzy blond hair; avid gardening—suggest her almost legendary status within the jazz community. The Bear's obvious relief in discovering that composing is hard work for the enigmatic Bley, clearly an artist he admires and respects, speaks further to the reputation she maintains as a serious artist, one who toils inexhaustibly over her craft.

Fiction aside, neither jazz histories nor histories of American music in general have included Carla Bley in their dominant narratives. Perhaps some of this inattention is due to her music's hovering in a gray space between appealing, accessible works and complex, avant-garde ones. Bley's music offers a staggering amount of variety, and for the most part, her compositional style is impossible to classify. She makes music that is vernacular yet sophisticated, appealing yet cryptic, joyous and mournful, silly and serious at the same time. Bley is full of contradictions, both when she talks about her music and when she composes. Her music takes us to jazz clubs but also to church, ballrooms, rock concerts, festival stages, punk dives, cabarets, and coffeehouses. She speaks many musical languages fluently—"like a mockingbird," as the bassist Charlie Haden, her lifelong friend, puts it—but holds citizenship papers in no one style.[1] She writes in many identifiable idioms of music with both respect and irreverence, yet she also composes original, idiosyncratic works that can be identifiable only as hers alone.

Bley is a prolific and influential American composer. And though her career, which began in the 1950s, has taken place largely within the venues and institutions of the jazz world, her music is often characterized as Third Stream, postmodernist, or just plain experimental, these labels due in part to her ability to write conventional big-band charts as well as classically influenced chamber works. Her compositions fall into a number of overlapping categories: lead sheets and short jazz tunes designed for improvising, completely notated and orchestrated chamber music, big-band ensemble parts, and larger works containing multiple connected parts (e.g., concept albums and suites). Her oeuvre varies widely in structure and style, from the eleven-beat-long *Walking Woman* to the monumental 105-minute "jazz opera" *Escalator over the Hill.* Much of her work explores unusual approaches to harmony, reveals a fondness for quotation, and revels in juxtapositions of tonal, tuneful textures with extended sections of chaotic freedom. A modest yet skilled pianist, Bley loves traditional instrumental combinations, such as the brass chorale, as well as bizarre sound effects (mechanical instruments, untrained voices singing, etc.). She moves fluidly between improvisational and nonimprovisational performance practices, in both traditional jazz and nonjazz contexts. Like any experienced bandleader, she displays a confident respect for the virtuosic players who bring her music to life. The results of all these ingredients are whimsical, baffling, entertaining, emotionally evocative, erudite, and profound.

Though Bley is first and foremost a composer, her career has taken many forms.[2] She is a pianist and organist (and occasional vocalist and saxophonist), bandleader, arranger, collaborator, organizer, and businesswoman. She has been called "Countess Basie" by her band members, who value her leadership, and "Bleythoven" by Steve Swallow, who points to her gifts as a composer. In a musical tradition historically dominated by African American men, the self-taught, self-effacing Caucasian Carla Bley is an anomaly in the world of jazz, especially as a bandleader.[3] This status alone suggests that Bley is worthy of study simply because she is unique. To be sure, an examination of her life and work can help us critically reexamine the role and historiographical treatment of women in jazz, but an "exceptional woman" strategy would sell her music short. Instead, this book offers a straightforward discussion of her life story and compositional style with the hope that it will stimulate deeper examinations of her work.

Bley herself says that questions about gender put her on the defensive. "When these subjects come up," she continues, "it's like acknowledging the existence of a problem that I refuse to even acknowledge, that I've never understood or felt."[4] Simply put, Bley has been an ongoing artistic presence over the past fifty years, and her historical significance stems from her contribution to key places, events, and groups in that history: the New York jazz club Birdland's golden years; the dawning of free jazz in the Los Angeles Hillcrest Club in the late 1950s; the October Revolution performances and the Jazz Composers Guild in New York during the 1960s; the Newport Jazz Festival of 1965; and the movements in jazz toward greater stylistic diversity (fusion, postmodernism, art rock, etc.) during the 1960s and 1970s. Since the earliest recordings of her music—by Paul Bley, Gary Burton, Art Farmer, Jimmy Giuffre, George Russell, and others—she has collaborated with many of the world's greatest musicians: Gato Barbieri, Jack Bruce, Don Cherry, Charlie Haden, Michael Mantler, John McLaughlin, Paul Motian, Dewey Redman, Roswell Rudd, Steve Swallow, and Tony Williams, to name just a few. Her ongoing work with Charlie Haden's Liberation Music Orchestra connects her to a culture of protest in American music. Her more classically oriented works have been written for and performed by musicians including Dennis Russell Davies, Keith Jarrett, and Ursula Oppens.

Like Charles Mingus before her, Bley is not only a composer and a bandleader but also a politically engaged activist who has taken professional matters—recording, publishing, and distributing—into her own hands for the sake of maintaining musical independence and professional control. Throughout her life Bley has sought artistic freedom. In this, Mingus might have been a model and an influence. She cofounded, with Michael Mantler, both a recording studio and a record label through which she has recorded and released all her own records since 1974. Bley and Mantler also cofounded the New Music Distribution Service, a historically significant nonprofit business in the tradition of the composer Henry Cowell's New Music enterprises (or any number of other avant-garde composer-driven publishing, recording, and distribution efforts throughout the twentieth century). She has also maintained a close partnership with the European label ECM Records for decades. Through the establishment of her own recording studio, record label, and distribution service, Bley has sustained an impressive amount of autonomy—a level of self-sufficiency rare for *any* American composer, let alone for an autodidactic composer-performer functioning in the profit-driven, corporation-dominated world of commercial jazz. Bley's activities in all these areas point further to the need for her presence in the histories of twentieth- and twenty-first-century American music.

I hope this first book on Carla Bley's life and works will help give both the long overdue scholarly attention and comprehensive treatment they deserve. Because of her inclusion in this serious yet accessible series, future students, musicians, and historians will find her among the company she deserves to keep, within the diverse pantheon of original American composers.

Note on Titles

Although it may seems at odds with standard typographical conventions, I italicize all the titles of Carla Bley's compositions so as not to differentiate hierarchically among pieces of differing lengths, instrumentation, or styles.

Note on Music

A few of Carla Bley's written compositions not readily available elsewhere are included here. However, many of the works discussed in this book can be viewed and downloaded at the official Carla Bley web site (see http://www.wattxtrawatt.com/leadsheetsbley.htm). A "suggested listening" list is included at the back of this book.

1 | *Walking Woman*

Oakland, New York,
Los Angeles, New York

I always did whatever interested me. I probably
would have compromised myself, but no one ever
asked me to.
  —Carla Bley

LIKE MANY SUCCESSFUL AUTODIDACTS, Carla Bley frequently
talks about the virtues of ignorance, the creative instincts that come from finding out things for oneself, both from necessity and by accident. Born Lovella
May Borg in Oakland, California, on May 11, 1936, to Christian fundamentalist
parents of Swedish descent, she received limited piano training from her father,
Emil Borg (1899–1990).[1] She had no formal music education beyond lessons
from beginning and intermediate piano method books. This relative underexpo-
sure to classical technique allowed her to develop an idiosyncratic musical language. Blessed with perfect pitch, she enjoyed music as a child and claims to have
played her first recital, with her fists, at age three. She was exposed to classical
music at home, as well as church music (ubiquitous Protestant church hymns,
such as "Rock of Ages," "Nearer My God to Thee," and "Power in the Blood of
the Lamb") at the nondenominational Havenscourt Colonial Church, where her
father worked as the organist and choirmaster. The church music in particular is
deeply ingrained in her compositional psychology, as it was, for example, in the
music of the American composer Charles Ives.

As a youngster Bley listened repeatedly to a recording she made from a radio
broadcast of the French composer Erik Satie's neoclassical ballet music *Parade*
(1917). She was exposed to the standard piano repertory—Beethoven, Chopin,

Grieg, Rachmaninov—through the lessons her father gave at home. She recalls her father using hymns to teach her how to play variations in different styles. Not surprisingly, as she recounts in any number of interviews, one of her earliest childhood compositions from this period was a set of variations on the tune "Onward Christian Soldiers." The variations, set by Bley as a waltz, a march, a polka, a dirge, and so on, foreshadowed her preference for these vernacular musical idioms in her later, more complex compositions. She also developed an ongoing interest in variation forms, a particularly important American vehicle for the musical practice of "signifying"—quoting, commenting, and expanding on preexisting material in personalized, rhetorical ways—which is central to the aesthetics of jazz.[2]

Overall, Bley's early musical training was fragmentary and unusual. Her parents' roles in this training, inadvertently perhaps, led to a great deal of independence for the young musician. "My music lessons continued until I was about seven. My father was exasperated by my lack of discipline and let my mother have a try at teaching me. Once, during a clash of wills, I bit her on the arm. They both gave up on me then, and I developed in my own unsupervised way."[3]

Bley's mother, Arline Anderson (1907–44), died when Bley was eight years old. Although tragic, the event seems to have nevertheless brought relief and solace to the young girl, who had endured many years of Arline's illness. A naturally independent child, she enjoyed a relatively unfettered childhood in the Foothill district of East Oakland. She continued composing: aside from composing the "Onward Christian Soldiers" variations, she remembers writing "some horrible cowboy song and the beginning of an opera set in the South Seas," which was perhaps a set of songs she began when she was about nine called *Over the Hill*.[4] She also played the piano at religious events and in local music competitions (though not all that successfully) and later accompanied rehearsals at a dance studio. As a teenager she turned her interest to roller skating. She felt that skating was another way of expressing musical ideas, and she particularly enjoyed the live organ accompaniment for her routines.[5] She competed in the California state championship and placed seventh in the freestyle category. This activity occupied her almost completely for about three years, during which time she graduated from Frick Middle School. After leaving the church around age fourteen, she dropped out of Castlemont High School, her attendance having dwindled to almost nothing. She had no further formal education. Bley unsuccessfully applied for a clerical job at a local Montgomery Ward (her typing was highly accurate but far too slow, she recalls) and then worked briefly in a music store selling sheet music. She also hung out and played music for entertainment in Berkeley cellar bars near campus. Somewhat oddly, given her geographical location, she remembers playing Ivy League college songs, including "The Bulldog Up at Yale Has No Tail" and "The Whiffenpoof Song."

Bley had little connection to the world of jazz at this time, though the San Francisco Bay Area hosted a number of lively clubs—the Purple Onion, the Black Hawk, and the hungry i, to name just a few. At a popular Oakland venue called the Burma Club, she heard (but claims not to have particularly responded to) several players who toured through the area. Dave Brubeck's quartet played frequently at the Burma Club and the Black Hawk during the 1950s. At some point she also heard Lionel Hampton's orchestra (the "Flying Home Band," she called it) play at an Oakland auditorium, and she has sometimes recalled this as the first jazz she heard. Bley's relatively late exposure to jazz and a lack of deliberately chosen models might be considered another contributing factor in her early development of a personal style. At age seventeen Bley took a job playing lounge piano in a Monterey nightclub called the Black Orchid. Enlisted men from nearby Fort Ord would surround her at the circular bar. Bley had limited improvising skills with only a modest repertoire, mostly of Tin Pan Alley tunes. She improvised only when she "played a mistake and had to recover": "I took a few jobs as a solo pianist in bars. I played a lot of beautiful standards, but my style was unspontaneous. The arrangements were figured out, note for note, in advance. Customers didn't like it much." Her particular relationship to improvisation, and her acceptance of "mistakes," has remained central to her creativity and to her approach toward performance. She told a *Down Beat* magazine critic in 1978: "I like to make mistakes, it makes me think up ways to correct them."[6]

Around this time Bley met and became romantically involved with a folksinger named Randy Sparks, who later formed the New Christy Minstrels. Her involvement with Sparks was probably her first significant collaborative musical relationship. She worked as his accompanist and wrote harmonic arrangements for his original melodies, and they frequently performed together at places such as the Purple Onion and the hungry i. Bley recalls: "He told me I should learn to play like Marian McPartland. Who was that? I didn't know much about jazz. I had been to a Lionel Hampton concert, and a friend had taken me to see Gerry Mulligan and Chet Baker at a nightclub, but I didn't understand what improvising was. That seemed like quite an obstacle."[7]

Sparks eventually traveled to San Diego to enlist in the navy. Soon thereafter Bley met a young man at the Black Orchid and decided to drive to New York with him. His father happened to be the Boston Symphony Orchestra concert-

8

master, and they took along a borrowed credit card and a loaf of bread. "The reason we did this," she said, "is because I wanted to go to Café Bohemia and hear Miles Davis."[8] Further, she had become fascinated by Teo Macero's *What's New?* (an album released in 1955), music that, in its approach toward harmony and improvisation, was more avant-garde and atonal than anything she had heard previously. Macero's music featured accordion, timpani, wordless vocalizations, and free, abstract, coloristic sections of music juxtaposed to more convention-ally swinging pieces. It was highly unusual for its time, especially in the degree to which it was composed and orchestrated, and it motivated Bley to learn more about modern jazz.

Recalling her first encounter with New York City, Bley has said: "I got there and went right to the Café Bohemia, and then my life really started."[9] She was most likely eighteen years old when she arrived in the city, which celebrated not only Miles Davis but also the brilliance of Charlie Parker, but it is not clear exactly when Bley first got there. She remembers standing outside a club, straining to hear Parker play; he died a short time later, on March 12, 1955 (Bley would turn nineteen that May). At the time, in myriad ways, the music industry was about to undergo drastic reorganization due to a "tectonic change," in the words of the Dutch economist and philosopher Wilfred Dolfsma, with popular music drenched in rock and roll coming to dominate the market fully during the 1960s and afterward.[10]

New to the city, Bley slept temporarily in Grand Central Station and then paid for an inexpensive hotel room near Times Square. She began working at the jazz clubs Basin Street and Birdland. At Birdland, which was located at the corner of Broadway and Fifty-second Street, she sold cigarettes and stuffed ani-mals. She occasionally worked as a photographer, too, taking pictures of couples in the audience. (Bley lied about her age by one or two years to be eligible for a cabaret card, necessary for employment in jazz clubs at the time.) For a budding composer, there was no better education than hearing the jazz artists who played at these clubs—Count Basie, John Coltrane, Miles Davis, Stan Getz, Dizzy Gil-lespie, Charles Mingus, Thelonious Monk, Anita O'Day, Bud Powell, Lester Young, and many others came through Birdland during its golden era, in the mid-to-late 1950s. Birdland, which had opened in 1949, was an epicenter of American music, and Bley had a front-row view, night after night. This opportunity allowed her ears to become finely tuned, and she received a first-rate education for free. It was there, probably at some point during 1956, that she met Paul Bley (b. 1932), the celebrated Canadian pianist. (Paul Bley's first record, *Introducing Paul Bley*, had been released on Charles Mingus's independent label Debut Records in 1953.) He bought a pack of cigarettes from her even though he did not smoke. They soon became a couple, and she traveled with him on a Canadian tour that included performances at the Cellar in Vancouver and the Penthouse/Windsor Steak House in Montreal, where "the sultry songstress Karen Borg" performed with him during the autumn of 1957.[11] Shortly after turning twenty-one, during the summer of 1957, she officially changed her name to Carla Borg (her father's middle name was Carl), with the unusual explanation on the correctional affidavit that the "incorrect name was added to the birth certificate at time of registration."[12]

Encouraged by Paul Bley, who recognized both her imaginative instinct for original musical ideas and her patience in working them out and writing them down, Carla Borg started composing regularly. The couple moved to Los Angeles, where, on August 21, 1957, Paul recorded an album (with the bassist Charlie Haden, the drummer Lennie McBrowne, and the vibraphonist Dave Pike) called *Solemn Meditation*, which included Borg's first mature composition, dated January 27, 1959. The work's title, *O Plus One*, was perhaps wordplay on the notion that this was her "Opus One." Borg also wrote the liner notes and took the cover photo of Paul Bley for this album.[13] After a brief separation, she and Bley were married in Sausalito, California, in the presence of her father. At this point she took the name Carla Bley, which she retains to this day.

During this period Paul Bley had a long-running engagement in Los Angeles at Hillcrest Club, on Washington Boulevard, performing with Haden, McBrowne, and Pike. Through a series of personnel changes, the band gradually transformed into a quintet consisting of Bley, Haden, Ornette Coleman on saxophone, Don Cherry on trumpet, and Billy Higgins on drums. Carla Bley listened to this new music intently, "like one huge ear": "I listened like I'm sure no musician could who played. I heard every note everybody played, every wart on every note everybody played. I'm sure that as a listener, I was unique."[14] She even recorded this music, with a hand-held tape recorder, on one occasion in October 1958. These tapes would be commercially released (as *The Fabulous Paul Bley Quintet* [America 30 AM 6120] and also as *Coleman Classics Vol. 1* [Improvising Artists IAI 373852]) and are now heralded as early documents of a poignant moment in the birth of a musical style that has since come to be known as "free jazz." Coleman also recorded several of his important early albums during this period in Los Angeles, including *Something Else!* (1958) and *Tomorrow Is the Question* (1959).

Carla Bley was further encouraged by musicians in Los Angeles. She recalls that the bassist Scott LaFaro liked to "warm up" with her piece *Donkey*, a fast chromatic twelve-bar blues. But perhaps most important, her encounter with Charlie Haden marked the start of a lifelong friendship, one that has resulted in some of the most innovative recordings ever made by large jazz ensembles, namely, the Liberation Music Orchestra projects beginning in 1969. Haden continually expresses profound respect for what he immediately identified as Carla's gifts: her intelligent ears and her unique musical vocabulary. From the beginning, they were "soul mates," he said, deeply connected as close friends and musical explorers, and they listened to music together extensively during this period.[15]

The Hillcrest Club quintet played much of Coleman's music, and some of Carla's as well; although accounts differ as to exactly how long the group survived, its radically new style of music apparently led the club to fire the band after about six weeks. All six musicians seem to have left California by mid-1959.[16] En route from Los Angeles to New York, the Bleys made a stop at the Lenox (Massachusetts) School of Jazz, where Jimmy Giuffre, Charles Mingus, George Russell, and others were participating in the school's summer performances. The Bleys snuck into concerts, slept on floors, and were treated with contempt for crashing the cafeteria. Nonetheless, this initial encounter with the clarinetist Giuffre would also become an important connection for Carla Bley.

Roswell Rudd, a Dixieland-playing trombonist fresh out of Yale, had come to New York City in 1958. He recalled a musical paradigm shift that occurred while the Bleys were in California, as exemplified by Miles Davis's sessions at Café Bohemia in the West Village:

> I stumbled in there one night, and there was the band—Miles had a saxophone player who had just that night come up from Philadelphia to start with him on this gig, and the saxophone player was John Coltrane. I was very much taken with the whole atmosphere. I kept going back that week. I was maybe sleeping over at [Steve] Lacy's loft on Bleecker Street. Café Bohemia was right off Sheridan Square in the West Village, downstairs. Everyone lined up at the bar; you could be real close to the band, standing up. I was really impressed by the atmosphere. Contrary to what Miles had going on in his recordings, this thing was very loose. He was just letting things happen. His drummer came sort of right at the end of the first set, so they played about three-quarters of the first set with no drums. That was really interesting. And when Philly Joe Jones got there, the sound changed. He was very strong. I guess he felt he had to make up for the forty minutes he missed. So that was my introduction to Miles Davis. The other thing about that was that he let Coltrane really have some space, and the thing that was remarkable about Coltrane was that he really put himself out there. He did not play slick saxophone. He was leaving himself open, and painting himself into corners and working his way out. It was almost as if he was making mistakes on purpose to see if he could then transcend his weaknesses. It was just amazing. We all stood at the bar with our jaws down because this guy was just so honest with what he was doing, and Miles was just letting it happen.[17]

The following year, 1959, witnessed the Ornette Coleman Quartet's debut performances at the Five Spot in November, as well as the releases of Coleman's *Shape of Jazz to Come*, Miles Davis's *Kind of Blue*, and John Coltrane's *Giant Steps* and the publication of George Russell's *Lydian Chromatic Concept of Tonal Organization*.[18]

That fall the Bleys met Steve Swallow (b. 1940), a young bassist who has remained one of Carla Bley's most important musical collaborators and closest friends up to the present day. The fateful meeting took place during a performance opportunity for Paul Bley at the pianist Ran Blake's second Bard College jazz festival, in 1959. Paul Bley had engaged the drummer Paul Cohen, who recommended hiring Swallow to complete the trio. Swallow was in his second year at Yale University, majoring in Latin American literature, but his encounter with Paul Bley and the freer style Bley was playing convinced him to devote his life to music. Swallow dropped out of school almost immediately and moved to New York, where he remained very close to the Bleys. At the time the couple lived in a tiny flat on East Ninth Street. Soon they moved to an apartment on the corner of Horatio and Hudson Streets in the northwest section of Greenwich Village, where they quickly became part of a burgeoning downtown music scene characterized by collaborative networking, cross-fertilization among the arts, constant activity despite a lack of resources, exploration of freer forms of improvisation, and workshop-type performances at small unconventional venues.

Central to the development of the "new thing" in jazz and its self-conscious move away from a bebop aesthetic were Ornette Coleman's debut performances at the Five Spot in November 1959 and at the Circle-in-the-Square Theater in 1960, as well as several radical recordings. In particular, his pianoless, double quartet album called *Free Jazz*, recorded on December 21, 1960, outraged much of the more traditional jazz community and announced something akin to a revolution in the way musicians conceptualized the relationships between the parts of a jazz improvisation. Free jazz differed from traditional jazz—even harmonically advanced bebop—in that it no longer relied on a steady beat and a harmonic (i.e., identifiable chord-based) structure over which a soloist would spontaneously create melodic elaborations. Performances of free jazz were not without structure and strategy, or preperformance planning by an ensemble, but the manner of expression liberated both the melody-playing soloist and the rhythm section to move in and out of a direct relationship to each other or to the "head"—that is, the music that begins and ends a work in small-ensemble jazz and that is usually composed by a member of the group. (Most of Bley's early compositions fall into the category of "free jazz head," since they were mostly short, rhythmic melodies meant to be used as loose frameworks for free group improvisation.) Since the 1920s, jazz composition and improvisation had mostly been based on either the twelve-bar blues or the thirty-two-bar popular song form typical of Tin Pan

Alley tunes; free jazz also liberated the structural forms of improvisation from the predictable strophic ("verse-chorus") form typical of jazz up to that point in time. The Atlantic Records release of Coleman's *Free Jazz* in 1961 included a reproduction of a Jackson Pollock painting (*White Light* [1954]), presumably to draw attention to the relationship between two seemingly formless, dynamic, anarchic, and intuitive new forms of spontaneous art.

Bley was encouraged by composers including George Russell, who lived nearby on Bank Street. Russell hired her as a transcriber and copyist, at seventy-five cents a page, for his 1961 album *Ezz-thetics* (which featured Eric Dolphy, Don Ellis, and Steve Swallow). At the same time, she continued writing short compositions that Paul Bley would frequently perform and record. She also read the recently published first edition of Russell's *Lydian Chromatic Concept*, his attempt to provide a theoretical framework for certain practices of improvisation. Bley claims to have "thrown in" to her new pieces a lot of sharp-eleventh chords—harmonies related to the Lydian scale on which Russell's method was based. She also wrote works for a group that Roswell Rudd called a "rehearsal band" and that included Archie Shepp on tenor saxophone. Around this time Bley applied for a scholarship to study at the Lenox School of Jazz, where Russell taught, but was turned down. (The school closed permanently in 1960.)

Alongside Paul Bley and George Russell, Steve Swallow, too, was particularly impressed with Carla Bley's compositions. He has remarked that aside from brief composition lessons at Yale and "learning the Monk repertory," knowing her music constituted "the only meaningful training in composition" he ever had.[19] As a result of his respect for her music, Swallow began sharing her compositions with all the musicians with whom he worked. It would be hard to overestimate the impact of this exposure on her growing reputation as an original composer, especially given how well connected Swallow was from around 1960 onward. Because of his advocacy and her husband's devotion to her creativity, within a few years Carla Bley's music was being performed and recorded not only by Paul Bley and George Russell but also by Gary Burton, Art Farmer, and Jimmy Giuffre.

Although during this time Bley continued working in the cloakroom of Basin Street and the Jazz Gallery (and visited a psychiatrist who advised her to become a seamstress rather than a composer), she also frequently played in Village coffeehouses. In May 1960 David Gordon opened Phase 2, at 302 Bleecker Street near Seventh Avenue, which was just across the street from the back door of the popular jazz club Sweet Basil, and it quickly became a popular venue for new jazz. Bley performed there, playing standards on solo piano or in a duo with Swallow for five dollars and a meal, Swallow recalls (see fig. 1).

Figure 1. Carla Bley, Steve Swallow, and Bill Folwell (others unknown) at Phase 2, Greenwich Village, early 1960s. Photographed by Paul Hoeffler. Used by permission of the Paul Hoeffler Estate.

These weekend jam sessions sometimes included the musicians Don Ellis and Bill Folwell. Bley remembers playing lots of Thelonious Monk tunes when she and Swallow performed with the saxophonist Steve Lacy and Roswell Rudd (the two had met at Yale during the 1950s); she also played the piano in the drummer Charles Moffett's group. Bill Dixon, a trumpet player, was a frequently appearing figure at Phase 2 as well, and he persuaded Dolphy, Lacy, Rudd, Cecil Taylor, and others to play there. Greenwich Village at the time teemed with similar venues, including the Take 3 Coffee House, MacDougal Street's Playhouse, and Le Figaro. Within little more than a year of returning to the "World's Capital of Jazz," the young Carla Bley was earning critical recognition as both a player and a composer in this tight-knit West Village community.[20] Soon her music would also be taken to an international audience, for the Jimmy Giuffre Trio (with Paul Bley and Steve Swallow) toured Europe in the fall of 1961, and she traveled with them. (She and Swallow recalled seeing a performance of Karlheinz Stockhausen's theatrical piece *Originale*, which was performed in October and November 1961 in Cologne and which may have influenced certain aspects of her later magnum opus *Escalator over the Hill*.) The trio made several recordings in 1961, including a live one in Graz, Austria, on October 27, that included several of her early compositions: *Ictus*, *Jesus Maria*, *In the Morning out There*, *Thesis*, and *Emphasis*.

During these first few years in New York, several other musicians in this circle covered her early compositions, including George Russell, who recorded *Bent Eagle*, *Dance Class*, and *Beast Blues* (all released in 1960; the liner notes for the first incorrectly calls Bley Russell's "student"), and the trumpet player Don Ellis, who recorded *Essence* and *Donkey*, both released in 1962. At over six-minutes long, *Bent Eagle* constituted her first extended recording; the liner notes to Russell's record *Stratusphunk*, on which it appeared, described it as a "delicate but firm piece, notable for a structure that permits almost unnoticeable transitions between composition and improvisation."[21] This balance between prescribed structure and individual expression would continue to be a primary concern in her compositional practice.

Paul Bley also made several other records between 1962 and 1965 that featured her music, including *Barrage* (1965), an album consisting entirely of her work. In his autobiography Paul recalled that during this time Carla worked earnestly on her compositions and that there was a symbiotic relationship between the ideas she developed through the process of piano playing and the exploration of those ideas through the craft of composition. Writing much later about the reasons for her early music's success, Carla Bley mused: "I guess it had a slightly different edge, due to my unorthodox background. I had managed to retain my ignorance, something you can never get back once you lose it."[22]

2 | *Sing Me Softly of the Blues*

Early Short Pieces
and *Songs without Words*

My first effort, a page of manuscript paper
absolutely covered with little black dots (without
stems), was criticized by my father for having too
many notes. So I erased most of them (and added
a few stems). From that point on I always tried to
leave a lot of space.
—Carla Bley, *The Music of Carla Bley*

FROM AN EARLY AGE Bley has placed considerable importance
on the idea of written music—that is, notation on paper. Having learned to read
music during her father's piano lessons while she was quite young, Bley was
intrigued by the existence of notated music and became curious about the people
who would create such a mysterious thing. She wondered whether or not she too
could do it. She often attributes her relative difficulty in improvising within a jazz
idiom to her primary attachment to reading notated music rather than to creating
spontaneously or reading chord symbols. She still writes all her music on paper
with a pencil, composing at a small upright piano in her home office. The act of
notating music has been central to her compositional experience.

As was outlined in the previous chapter, Bley's earliest extant compositions
date from the period of her relationship with Paul Bley, and several of these
pieces were written at his request and recorded by him on multiple occasions.
(In fact, between 1958 and 1966 Paul Bley made at least twenty-nine recordings
of Carla Bley's early work.) These pieces tend to be short miniatures, a "tiny
snippet of an idea"—or "haiku style," as the composer herself has called them,
referring to their often austere nature and poetic brevity.[1] Steve Swallow has
described them as "little distilled songs containing a single, specific idea."[2] Much
of her compositional style during this period was directly influenced by the fact

that Paul Bley wanted something more radical than traditionally organized song forms over which to improvise freely. As a result, none of these short early pieces were meant to be performed as fixed compositions read verbatim off the score. Rather, they were intended to be treated as composed jazz material is generally treated. They included short heads used as springboards for free improvisations and cyclic "songs," whose longer verse-chorus structures would be repeated several times. Many of these pieces, such as *King Korn* (which she wrote for Sonny Rollins, though he never played it), were originally used for free improvisations but took on a stronger compositional profile when she later reworked them. Bley could compose something like *King Korn* quickly (in about twenty minutes, she claims), but the arrangements would take her much longer. (Much later, on the album she made with Swallow titled *Are We There Yet?* [1999], Bley exploited the strong rhythmic profile of *King Kong* by quoting George Gershwin's well-known tune "I've Got Rhythm" near the end of the arrangement.) Bley rearranged many of these miniatures into fixed compositions with improvisation built into the composed structure, and many survive in multiple versions on her and others' recordings of her early work, from the 1960s up to the present day.

According to Bley, her earliest mature work is the twelve-bar blues in F called *Donkey*, which she probably composed in Los Angeles in 1958. In a collection of her piano music published in 1981, Bley called the melody of the piece "a blues line," even though it flies by at a rapid pace (with a quarter note equal to 176 beats per minute) and seems more akin to bebop melodies than to anything else. It follow the standard twelve-bar blues harmonic pattern, unlike her frequently recorded *Sing Me Softly of the Blues* (1962), which is a fourteen-bar cycle (plus an introduction and a coda). For *Donkey* she instructs the player to improvise "in the traditional manner" and states that the left-hand part "should be changed to fit the style of the player." Likewise, the short explosion of *Ictus* (also dated 1958) is to be played "as fast as possible."

Unlike *Donkey*, which she considered a blues, *Ictus* does not have chord symbols written in the way then standard for jazz scores. Bley has published the piece both with and without bar lines and with differing interpretations of the rhythmic feel (see fig. 2; the metered version of *Ictus* can be seen at http://www.wattxtrawatt.com/leadsheetsbley.htm).[3] Many of her early works have a tendency to obscure any sense of metrical regularity through irregular placements of short phrases, held notes (ties) across the bar lines, and plenty of rests. The catchy phrase-rest pattern at the beginning of *Ictus* sounds like a phrase with beats divided into alternating groups of two and five, for example, but in one printing of the piece is notated as alternating groups of three and four. Perhaps tellingly, in her notes

ICTUS

BY CARLA BLEY

Figure 2. *Ictus* (without barlines). *Carla Bley, Vol. 1: Early Short Pieces (1958–1964)*. Copyright 1976, Alrac Music. Used by permission of Carla Bley.

to the later publication of *Ictus*, the composer instructs: "Use this piece to open and close a freely improvised solo or series of solos. After learning the written material, disregard the bar lines, squeeze the phrases together and accelerate the middle section." Her *Walking Batterie Woman*, which combines titles and ideas from two earlier pieces (*Walking Woman* and *Batterie*), similarly resisted traditional notation, and Bley was unable to rework it into conventional notation with metrical markings. She wrote: "Follow the phrase markings and play the notes very

17

close together in the sections without bar lines." She also felt it necessary to add a rhythmic clarification: "The groups of three attached notes are not triplets."

Paul Bley enhanced his repertoire by playing an assortment of these short pieces, including *Around Again, King Korn, Syndrome, Vashkar, Batterie,* and certainly the most enduring of these early works, *Ida Lupino. Ictus* and *Ida Lupino* clearly represent two sides of the Carla Bley coin, a duality Igor Stravinsky referred to as the Dionysian and Apollonian sides of a composer's personality: the Dionysian side is marked by subjective expressivity and wild abandon, while the Apollonian side is characterized by cool balance and restrained objectivity.[4] In Bley's early work, the former is fiery, quick, and nervous, with irregular and asymmetrical rhythmic phrases and chromatic or even atonal pitch material. The latter tends to be smooth and lyrical, dominated by a simple repetitive melody, tonal or modal harmonies, slower tempos, and a calm demeanor. Where the former is unpredictable and sometimes without pulse, the latter is highly patterned and repetitive.

Works reflecting Bley's Dionysian personality include *King Korn, Ictus,* and *Vashkar,* while those showing her Apollonian personality include *Ida Lupino* (and its odd musical mirror image, *Oni Puladi*), *Vox Humana,* and *New Hymn.* Other short works, such as *Ad Infinitum* and *Around Again,* generally fall into the repetitive, tonal category, though they are more up-tempo pieces. Most of the more lyrical pieces were self-published later in a collection titled *Songs without Words* (1961–75), probably in reference to Felix Mendelssohn's mid-nineteenth-century piano collections of the same name.[5] Both the static and lyrical songlike ballads and the chromatic and jerky off-the-cuff phrases might reflect Bley's early interest in the music of the French composer Erik Satie or the influence of Thelonious Monk. Like Bley, both these composers could write memorable melodies as well as strong irregular rhythmic motives. All Bley's work since this period has been enhanced by these two fundamental skills. By coupling them with the later development of her gifts for orchestration and for managing large-scale sonic architecture, she took control of the elements most central to her compositional career.

Songs without Words constitutes volume 2 of what one might call the Carla Bley songbook. Bley's volume 1, *Early Short Pieces (1958–1964),* includes a number of the most compositionally unique of these miniatures and represents at a glance the fluid spectrum of her young compositional personality. All these works are scored for solo piano, though ensembles both small and large have recorded arrangements of each. None takes up more than a page, and some include just a single line of music. *Floater* is merely a series of parallel chords, one ascending pair, in eighth notes, per five-beat measure (see fig. 3). Excluding repetitions and

Figure 3. *Floater. Carla Bley, Vol. 1: Early Short Pieces (1958–1964)*. Copyright 1976, Alrac Music. Used by permission of Carla Bley.

octave transpositions, this entire piece is made up of three one-beat gestures that seem to float, as the title suggests, on their nearly empty staves.

Walking Woman is also striking in its brevity, though its harmony, if one can call it that, is more varied than that in *Floater*. The piece consists of one system of music, with a repeat sign encompassing the entire phrase (see fig. 4). Bley eschews certain notational conventions, not only omitting time signatures, key signatures,

19

Figure 4. *Walking Woman. Carla Bley, Vol. 1: Early Short Pieces (1958–1964)*. Copyright 1976, Alrac Music. Used by permission of Carla Bley.

and bar lines but also leaving out rests that would normally fill the unarticulated space when one hand rests while the other plays. The rhythm is asymmetrical and constantly varied, and with the help of strategically placed eighth notes, the eleven-beat pattern shifts off the pulse midphrase. Briefly syncopated, it shifts back on at beat ten. The leaping chromatic bass line is unusual, in part because of the "missing" rests: it looks as if it comprises only six beats, not the right-hand part's eleven. Evoking the Austrian modernist Anton von Webern in its brevity and concision,

Walking Woman is a succinct compositional gesture that demonstrates the development of Bley's melodic, harmonic, and rhythmic language. Much of its surprise and its energy can be heard in her later work as well, specifically, in *Romantic Notions*, a collection of more classically oriented solo piano pieces (see chapter 9).

Several other pieces published in this collection, in particular *Violin* and *Closer*, are also notable for their unconventional approach to notation. These too lack key signatures, meters, and bar lines (see fig. 5). They include thick, horizontal

Figure 5. *Violin. Carla Bley, Vol. 1: Early Short Pieces (1958–1964)*. Copyright 1976, Alrac Music. Used by permission of Carla Bley.

lines rather than conventional rhythmic notation to represent long-held notes or chords in the left hand.

Similarly, *Generous 1* reveals Bley's interest in nonstandard, or synthetic, scales. These pieces also draw attention to Bley's impressionistic tastes, for they seem to focus on washes of harmonic color rather than on particular progressions or temporal relationships. Charlie Haden has made a point of comparing Bley's harmonic language to that of early twentieth-century French composers associated with impressionism, including Claude Debussy, Maurice Ravel, Erik Satie, and Darius Milhaud.[6] Bley's harmonic experimentation is consistent as well with developments in modern jazz at the time. One of the defining organizational features of jazz composition up to around 1960 had been the chord progression, called the "changes," which moved according to defined relationships. Bley's early work often lacks anything remotely resembling changes. Pieces such as *Violin* and *Closer* bear the influence of Ornette Coleman, whose contributions to the free-jazz revolution included liberating and foregrounding the melody rather than allowing the chord changes to determine the form and an improviser's melodic choices. A further connection to Coleman's work around this time is Bley's emphasis on changing scales, or pitch collections, within a short amount of time (creating a sometimes jarring effect), thus increasing unpredictability. In addition, Bley frequently subverts the listeners' expectations further through a series of asymmetrical, rhythmically varied phrases of differing lengths.

Thematic unity nonetheless also appears in Bley's early pieces. *Closer* coheres through a frequently repeated ascending motive always placed in the same portion of the piano treble range; *Violin*, marked *rubato*, is formally organized by the repetition of two brief phrases, each consisting of just a few beats, followed by a chromatic closing line. This piece takes less than a minute to play, but its form might be summed up as ABABC. The final chord is not a typical resolution for pieces within a jazz tradition based on specific tonal rules but would be typical in the playing of Thelonious Monk, for example. *Generous 1* also repeats scalar phrases as a way of organizing the composition. These brief pieces sound improvisatory, as if they were made up on the spot, yet they are carefully planned and organized compositions, whatever their lengths.

Similarly, *And Now, the Queen*, a composition Steve Swallow considers among Bley's finest works, reveals many of the previously mentioned characteristics in the form of a repeated four-bar melody that changes meter every bar (see fig. 6). A fermata stops the melodic motion after seven beats, enhancing a free-time feel to the piece. The melody is unified by an initial descending phrase that sounds strongly tonal (a major third is repeated three times right before this melody

Figure 6. *And Now, the Queen*. *Carla Bley, Vol. 1: Early Short Pieces (1958–1964)*. Copyright 1976, Alrac Music. Used by permission of Carla Bley.

is heard again). Bley composed the piece without a key signature, even though there are only three brief instances of notes outside the key of G-flat. Again, no traditional harmonic structure is to be found here; in fact, this melody almost lacks accompaniment altogether. The final chord seems to have little to do with the opening melody, yet the chromatic flavor presented here is effectively more lyrical than jarring. This sparse, impressionistic harmony is probably part of what made these pieces so appealing to other players, in particular composers, such as

George Russell, who were exploring the possibility of increased harmonic stasis and thus contributed to the growing practice of modal jazz.

Unlike *Violin, Closer, Generous 1,* and *And Now, the Queen,* Bley's *Flags* seems relatively tonal or at least modal, though again, the left-hand accompaniment is so thin and infrequent that it is difficult to speak of harmonic motion at all (see fig. 7). *Flags* also contains a direct quotation of the "Star-Spangled Banner," though the opening notes of that melody are displaced, scattered in dif-

Figure 7. *Flags. Carla Bley, Vol. 1: Early Short Pieces (1958–1964).* Copyright 1976, Alrac Music. Used by permission of Carla Bley.

ferent octaves and divided between the hands in a syncopated manner so as to impede the listener's recognition of this familiar and meaning-laden tune. (In the late 1970s, both *And Now, the Queen* and *Flags* would appear prominently in Bley's medley-like America-themed suite called *Spangled Banner Minor*.) Similar in style to *Flags* is the very fast eight-bar *Around Again*. This piece consists of a fragmentary melody interrupted by fast chromatic flourishes. The "accompaniment" in the first three bars consists merely of several isolated low notes. These bass notes, though hardly amounting to a bass line, serve as the tonal axis for this short piece. The surprising jolts within such a small amount of musical space help make Bley's early work so stimulating. These "haiku," distinguished by their unpredictability, balance the smooth static repetitions of Bley's more lyrical or metrical pieces, such as *Ida Lupino* and *Syndrome*, both of which immediately establish a regular pulse and predictable rhythmic motives that continue through to the end.

Though *Ictus* appears to be a close second, no Bley composition has been played more by other artists than *Ida Lupino*, which Bley copyrighted in 1963 and later published in *Songs without Words* (for the lead sheet, see http://www.wattxtrawatt.com/leadsheetsbley.htm). First recorded by Paul Bley on his album *Turning Point* in 1964, this memorable piece has been recorded dozens of times since. The musical content of Bley's enduring work, named for the famous actress and director from the 1930s and 1940s, is startlingly simple. Anchored by a G in the bass throughout, the melody repeats a pattern as spare and as impossible to forget as the opening motive of Beethoven's Fifth Symphony. Outlining the simple melody, she repeats the work-defining, straight (not swung) pattern (short–short–short–short–long–long) every four bars. The melody itself is characterized by a wealth of repeated pitches, causing some critics to compare the tune to an unskilled child trying to pick out a simple melody on a piano with one finger. It could also be interpreted as representing Bley's own declarations of inadequacy as a pianist throughout much of her career (the simplicity of the melody is particularly emphasized in Bley's recording of the solo piano introduction to the piece on her 1977 album *Dinner Music*). There is nothing virtuosic about *Ida Lupino*. Understated, modest, direct, and transparent, it demonstrates an extreme economy of means foreign not only to bebop and free jazz but to nearly all styles of Western music during the early 1960s. (Bley's tonal, repetitive "songs without words" pre-date Terry Riley's landmark work of early tonal, pulsed minimalism, *In C* [1964], by several years.) With its continual G drone in the bass, *Ida Lupino* is harmonically modest. The melody's strategic placement often creates a subtle sense of tension against crucial notes in the chords.

By 1962 approximately one dozen albums that included arrangements and interpretations of Bley's early works had been released by prominent recording artists (she herself has retained some of the early pieces within her own work). One of her most successful early works, *Jesus Maria* (1961), was recorded by Jimmy Giuffre almost immediately after she wrote it, and it was later turned into a virtuosic orchestration for the Carla Bley Band's recording *Musique Mecanique* in 1978. The lazy, lyrical opening melody, somewhat reminiscent of Miles Davis's "Flamenco Sketches," contrasts with a middle section dominated by a rhythmic pattern of three, three, and two in the bass, which gives the section a Latin feel. The original piece is a written-out ABABA song form. The version she orchestrated for the 1978 album is a twelve-minute rondolike romp around the original tune peppered with "Other Spanish Strains." *Jesus Maria* also appears in an extended arrangement on her 2009 *Carla's Christmas Carols* album.

In a more subtle way, the beginning of another early piece, *Vashkar* (1963), makes a prominent appearance at the beginning of *Rawalpindi Blues*, one of the most powerful songs culminating the last section of the album *Escalator over the Hill* (1968–71). The five-note opening phrase of *Vashkar*, outlining a B-minor scale, appears to be what gave shape and motion to the syllabic singing of the words "Rawalpindi blues" (short–short–short–long–long). The reworking of key early source material for her later compositions for large ensembles has provided Bley ample opportunities to continually redefine her relationship to her own past creativity. This body of early work would become significant for the music to follow in that it provided a foundation from which to build a rhythmic and harmonic language, an approach toward orchestration, and an ongoing exploration of large and small forms.

3 | *Social Studies*

The Jazz Composers Guild and the Jazz Composers Orchestra

BY 1964 THE BLEYS' circle of friends included not only Steve Swallow and the members of the Ornette Coleman quartet but also the bassist Gary Peacock and his wife, Annette (who would later become Paul Bley's second wife). The poet and jazz enthusiast Paul Haines, whom Carla Bley possibly met as a fellow audience member at Mingus concerts and at whose house she met Roswell Rudd, also socialized in this circle, along with Haines's wife, the painter Jo Hayward Haines. The friends met frequently to discuss the current and future state of jazz, in tandem with a larger group that included Bill Dixon, Cecil Taylor, Roswell Rudd, Sonny Murray, and Albert Ayler. A crisis within the jazz community seemed imminent. The early to mid-1960s saw great changes not only in the styles of playing jazz but in the way jazz was perceived. These changes happened alongside an undeniable decline in the widespread consumption of jazz as "popular" music meant as entertainment. Ornette Coleman, John Coltrane, Charles Mingus, Cecil Taylor, and Lennie Tristano, among other pioneers, had initiated a shift in artistic attitudes among jazz composers, one that took them away from the situation wherein, as Timothy Marquand was quoted saying in the *New York Times*, "in a night club, a musician is basically a liquor salesman."[1] During the 1960s jazz stood on shaky ground. Rock, R&B, and soul stole audiences, while the Five Spot and other important venues eventually went out of business.

Record companies increasingly wanted to record only what they knew could sell. Musicians' and composers' collectives tried to take matters into their own hands by founding new venues and producing their own concerts with a view to maintaining artistic control. Some scholars have connected these market factors to the creation, during the 1960s, of the Jazz Composers Guild and the Jazz Composers Orchestra Association in New York, the Association for the Advancement of Creative Musicians (AACM) in Chicago, the Black Artists' Group in St. Louis, and other composer collectives established for the purpose of performing, recording, and disseminating avant-garde jazz composition. These efforts were not new in the world of jazz, however; by this time composers including Dave Brubeck, Ornette Coleman, Duke Ellington, Dizzy Gillespie, Fletcher Henderson, Charles Mingus, Sun Ra, and Max Roach had made efforts to take control of some of the business aspects of their careers. Nonetheless, such initiatives became more concentrated and collaborative during the mid-1960s.

The trajectory of Carla Bley's career was directly affected by her involvement with one such effort in New York City during the autumn of 1964, namely, the "October Revolution in Jazz," a series of avant-garde jazz performances organized by Bill Dixon at the Cellar Café, on West Ninety-first Street, a venue owned by Dixon's friend Peter Sabino. The series resulted in Dixon's establishing an organization called the Jazz Composers Guild, a member-run musicians' cooperative. Composers involved in the guild considered it to be vitally important in combating a sense of isolation among progressive musicians during this period of shifting audience demographics. Though short-lived, this organization proved to be the most consequential pre-AACM effort aimed at total composer-controlled self-determination. Later in 1964 the Jazz Composers Guild produced a series of events similar to Dixon's "October Revolution" called "Four Days in December" and held at Judson Hall, on West Fifty-seventh Street. This concert included music by Bley and by some of the leading avant-garde jazz composers of the time, all of whom were founding members of the guild. The first night featured the Cecil Taylor Unit and the Bill Dixon Sextet; the second night showcased the Paul Bley Quintet and the "Jazz Composers Guild Orchestra," with works by Michael Mantler and Carla Bley; the third night featured the Archie Shepp Quartet and the Free Form Improvisation Ensemble; and the final night presented "Le Sun-Ra Arkestra" and the Roswell Rudd–John Tchicai Quartet (the New York Art Quartet). Advance tickets cost two dollars at the Jazz Record Center and Sam Goody record shops and at Roswell Rudd's Chambers Street apartment, the organization's official address.

The Jazz Composers Guild acknowledged their music as a branch of non-commercial, avant-garde art music in desperate need of subsidy and aimed to find support through foundation grants. The guild included Dixon, the Bleys, Sun Ra (who strongly opposed Carla Bley's membership in the group because she was a woman), Rudd, Mantler, Taylor, Tchicai, John Winter, Burton Greene, and Shepp.[2] Set against the backdrop of escalating civil rights conflicts, the guild held collective self-determination as a founding idea—it prescribed a set of rules according to which individual performances and recording offers were subjected to a group decision-making process akin to that of a labor union, which often led to competitive animosity and conflict. The guild soon collapsed under the weight of strong individual creative egos, for its members were unable to put their own personalities and needs aside for the sake of a greater common good. More positively, however, Carla Bley and Michael Mantler drew on the guild to develop what Roswell Rudd has called an "all-star" band; they created the Jazz Composers Guild Orchestra because having a band was a requirement of being in the guild. (Only Bley and Mantler failed this requirement before joining.) Bley wrote what could be considered her first large work for the Jazz Composers Guild Orchestra, a twelve-minute composition called *Roast*, which was presented by the ensemble (a fifteen-person group, including herself, by 1965) during the "Four Days in December" concerts. A "workshop performance" followed over three nights in April 1965. The "Four Days in December" performance of *Roast* was recorded and released on a record called *Communication* and issued by Fontana. Bley has not made a score of *Roast* available, but in a *Down Beat* article from around this time, Don Heckman wrote: "Some of the music played by the Jazz Composers Guild Orchestra—especially the works of Mike Mantler and Carla Bley—is not notated very differently from that of Cage, Christian Wolff, and Earle Brown."[3]

The Jazz Composers Guild's competition for audiences was stiff in New York City during the mid-1960s. Stars such as Charles Mingus, Horace Silver, and Coleman Hawkins regularly held sway at the Village Vanguard, the Half Note, the Five Spot, and similar venues. The guild nonetheless attempted to establish a new performance space with a new aesthetic. Their main concert location, the Contemporary Center, was located in Edith Stephen's dance studio. Typically, each group connected to the Jazz Composers Guild would perform in the space over several successive nights; Bley and Mantler's Jazz Composers Guild Orchestra performed for three nights in April. Reached via a creaky flight of stairs, Stephen's studio, which the guild rented for its concerts, was a small triangular room with a low ceiling located two floors above the Village Vanguard, on

South Seventh Avenue near Eleventh Street. Its location in the same building as the legendary jazz club made the venue problematic. On occasion, fellow avant-gardist Ornette Coleman might be scheduled to play on the better-known stage in the cellar while his friend and colleague Paul Bley fought to draw an audience to the experimental space two floors up. While putting away folding chairs after one of these concerts, Carla Bley and Mantler met Timothy Marquand, an independently wealthy amateur musician and jazz fan who, after studies at Harvard University, was earning a degree in music theory at the Mannes School of Music. Marquand, who considered Bley "honest, inspirational, and funny" and who loved her music, would soon come to play a key administrative role in Bley and Mantler's future endeavors.[4]

In 1965, during this period of increasing scarcity of resources for jazz musicians—fewer venues, smaller audiences, more selective record producers, and rock and roll's increasing dominion over the market—the National Endowment for the Arts was established, though NEA grant programs in jazz were not inaugurated until 1970. At that time the agency began tentatively to invest money in jazz composers, who for several decades had been insisting on the integrity of their work as national products of cultural value by living American artists. (Later in her career Bley applied for an NEA jazz grant and was told that her work was not jazz; she was advised to apply to the "serious" music division instead.) The New York *Art* Quartet (emphasis mine), a group founded in 1963 by Roswell Rudd and John Tchicai, aimed to address this division between jazz and art music, as did the Art Ensemble of Chicago several years later.

From the start, a number of other people became involved with Jazz Composers Guild activities, helping to build an interdisciplinary community of creative forces. The Canadian-born artist and musician Michael Snow became an important friend to the guild, and he made his downtown loft available as a rehearsal space. A jazz pianist of professional quality, Snow was deeply invested in the new improvised music, particularly free jazz. In 1964, the same year as the "October Revolution" concerts, he made a short film, *New York Eye and Ear Control*, that used a free-jazz soundtrack featuring Albert Ayler, Don Cherry, John Tchicai, Roswell Rudd, Gary Peacock, and Sonny Murray (with Paul Haines as recording engineer); the soundtrack was later released, under the same name, as an Albert Ayler recording. Snow also produced artwork that used an image of Carla Bley's silhouette and contributed it to the album (he called the piece *Walking Woman*, a title she later adopted for one of her briefest miniatures); he produced artwork for Paul Bley's record *Barrage* as well. Several of these recordings, including *Barrage* and *New York Ear and Eye Control*, were released on ESP-Disk records, a label that had been founded by Bernard Stollman. A lawyer associated with the guild, Stollman sometimes provided legal representation for Ornette Coleman and Cecil Taylor.

The Jazz Composers Guild presented its final event in April 1965 and then dissolved. Later that summer, however, the second day of the Newport Jazz Festival included an afternoon concert billed as "The New Thing in Jazz: A Study of the Avant-Garde." Leonard Feather served as master of ceremonies for the concert, which looked much like a Jazz Composers Guild delegation and included sets by the guild ensemble, now renamed the "Jazz Composers Orchestra" (with music by Mantler and Bley); the Archie Shepp Trio; the Paul Bley Quartet; and Cecil Taylor's group. That evening Art Blakey, Carmen McRae, Miles Davis, Thelonious Monk, and John Coltrane performed in a concert called "Jazz for Moderns." The 1965 festival—which somewhat incongruously included Pete Seeger and Frank Sinatra, as well as Earl Hines, Stan Getz, the Count Basie Orchestra, and many others—marked the only occasion on which this legendary festival included music from the avant-garde/free-jazz scene. (June 1965's parallel Newport Folk Festival saw Bob Dylan plugging his guitar into an electric amplifier, much to the chagrin of Pete Seeger, not to mention the audience.)

The Newport festival's program booklet aimed to be educational, reprinting an article entitled "They Don't Call It Jazz: The Moody Men Who Play the New Music," which served as an introduction to "the disturbing sounds" of Taylor, Coleman, Ayler, Peacock, and several others who "played the music, not the background," as Coleman put it.[5] In their reviews of the "New Thing in Jazz" concert, the jazz critics Feather and Dan Morgenstern remarked that the audience was one of the smallest they had ever seen at Newport, but an article published in the *Toronto Telegram* said that the performers "held spellbound a small, but the most attentive audience of the festival." That same author described Bley as appearing "in a man's shirt, smoking a pipe."[6] Morgenstern commented: "Mrs. Bley's writing was considerably more skillful than Mantler's, achieving more varied textures from the ensemble."[7] Shortly before the festival, one of the first feature-length articles about Bley and her music appeared in an April 1965 issue of the *New York Herald Tribune*. It pointed out that she published her own music through Alrac Music Company (Alrac is Carla spelled backward) and that she often used "lines and boxes" rather than traditional notation to graphically communicate her music.

Around the time when the Jazz Composers Guild collapsed, the Bleys' marriage also came to an end. Carla Bley soon formed a new partnership, and subsequent twenty-five-year marriage, with the Austrian trumpet player Michael Mantler. Born in Vienna in 1943, Mantler had come to the United States in

1962 to study at the Berklee College of Music. He worked in Boston with the pianist Lowell Davidson before moving to New York City in September 1964; once there, he became involved with the "October Revolution" concerts and the Jazz Composers Guild. After the 1965 Newport Festival, Bley and Mantler went on a European tour with Steve Lacy, Kent Carter on bass, and Aldo Romano on drums. The quintet called themselves Jazz Realities, and their tour resulted in an eponymously titled recording made in Holland on January 11, 1966. (Bley was about seven months pregnant at the time of recording.) The album includes five of her original compositions.

Jazz Realities is an important source, for it is the earliest available documentation of Bley as a performer.[8] Her jerky and interrupted phrasing—quick, short, thin-textured statements—is displayed well on the first track, *Doctor*, a piece she wrote in Vienna during the tour. The performance opens with Lacy and Mantler presenting the main theme in tandem. Within thirty seconds the front men have dropped out completely and the pianist-composer takes over, playing a captivating yet sparse solo that in its one and one-half minutes reveals Bley to be anything but a mediocre pianist. She herself has claimed pianistic mediocrity at many points throughout her career, repeatedly drawing attention to her ambivalent relationship with her instrument and to her primary identification as a composer. Her solo playing on *Doctor* is almost completely monophonic, rarely sounding more than one note at a time. It avoids vertical relationships almost entirely, except when it coincides fleetingly with the bass line. The solo sounds as if she was dividing the melodic line between her two hands, much in the style of Thelonious Monk. As is the case with many of her early compositions, her emphasis on the linear in this improvisation is not challenged by a foundation based on chords. Much of her playing bears the marks of both Monk (in the jerky phrasing, empty space, sharply articulated attacks, etc.) and Coleman (who foregrounded melodic invention), and perhaps also a bit of Cecil Taylor when she thickens the texture into clustery runs near the end of her solo.

The record also features the more lyrical, static side of her musical personality in the recording of *Oni Puladi* (a literal musical retrograde of *Ida Lupino*). Reversing the memorable pattern of four short notes and two long ones that gives *Ida Lupino* its melodic identity, *Oni Puladi* focuses on the dronelike long-held note that seems to grin mysteriously in the face of the hyperactivity of a piece such as *Doctor*. Again the fluid playing of Mantler and Lacy gives this interpretation a sensitivity that sheds new light on the beauty of both the original composition and its strangely reversed sibling. Bley's solo in the middle of the recording almost completely stops all action, making the listener notice how static the piece is. The main melody is all the more beautiful for having disappeared completely during her few moments alone with it.

On their return from the Jazz Realities tour, Bley and Mantler devoted their energy to developing the Jazz Composers Orchestra (JCO). They defined this group as a working ensemble for which ambitious composers could try out large works of greater scope. In addition, they embraced the independence of their enterprise as an opportunity to determine for themselves "what the ratio of written to improvised music is."[9] Bley has called this trend of musicians taking matters into their own hands a "social miracle," one that liberated them fully from the impositions of corporate record producers.[10] Joseph Papp's Public Theater, on Lafayette Street, became one of the JCO's most important venues. Timothy Marquand, who had been introduced to Bill Dixon by Cecil Taylor and who had been involved marginally with the Jazz Composers Guild, became a patron and administrator for the enterprise (he also supported the orchestra financially and later acted as something of a benefactor to Bley). In 1966 Bley and Mantler chartered the Jazz Composers Orchestra Association (JCOA) as a not-for-profit organization formed to produce concerts and recordings. Marquand served as president and Mantler served as executive director. A creative, well-organized, and successful fundraiser, Mantler conducted most of the administrative business during the lifetime of the JCOA. Marquand became an outspoken and eloquent advocate for the organization, equating the work of the Jazz Composers Orchestra to that of the greatest of America's creative "rebels": Herman Melville, Charles Ives, Jackson Pollock, Martha Graham, Charlie Parker, Ornette Coleman, and Cecil Taylor.[11]

In 1966 Mantler and Bley had a daughter, Karen Mantler. The new mother was celebrated with her first *Down Beat* International Critics Poll award. Also that year, Bley was hired to write piano arrangements for a Christmas songbook called *A Wealth of Carols* (Mantler contributed copying work for the publication), in which she included her composition *Jesus Maria*, with lyrics she wrote for this occasion. To date Bley had written approximately thirty-five compositions, most of which had been recorded—some multiple times by many different artists—and for which she earned royalties. Nonetheless, the inclusion of *Jesus Maria* in this obscure little Christmas carol book constituted her first publication. She was thirty years old and on the brink of her most startlingly original work.

4 | "Mad at Jazz"

A Genuine Tong Funeral

BLEY TOOK PART IN a second European tour in 1967, playing what she called "high energy hateful screaming music" with the West German free improvisers Peter Brötzmann and Peter Kowald. At the time, partly because of the aggressiveness of this music, she felt "mad at jazz."[1] Not only was Bley growing ambivalent about the expressive qualities of free jazz, but she started to question her relationship to the African American roots of jazz. She began cultivating a musical alliance with what she considered to be her true culture: European and European American music. In particular, she had lost her tolerance for long solos full of emphatic self-expression. With this significant change in attitude, she felt as if she experienced the beginning of a new musical life. Coinciding with these reevaluations, her friend Michael Snow introduced her to the Beatles' newest record, *Sergeant Pepper's Lonely Hearts Club Band*, which had been released on the first day of June 1967, on the eve of the so-called Summer of Love. Snow told Bley that many visual artists were already listening to this record instead of the avant-garde jazz they had tended to favor in the past. In particular, Bley remembers Snow playing her the album's last song, "A Day in the Life," and being astounded by what she heard. The sonic adventurousness of the album and the audacity of its larger musical architecture impressed her. The "concept album," a record beyond a set of short, unrelated songs, suggested an intriguing possibility for Bley. Formal plans were fundamental to her compositional designs, as is evident in her claim that she needed "a lot of order" and that she was "a very conservative person."[2]

Under the influence of this new thinking, she began developing ideas for a large-scale project based on work she had begun as early as 1964. She was unable to interest a record company in this project, but when Steve Swallow mentioned it to his current bandleader, the vibraphonist Gary Burton, Bley's luck changed. (At this point, Swallow, having been infected with what he calls a lifelong "virus of Carla's music," had for many years been showing her compositions to everyone he encountered.)[3] Burton enjoyed almost complete autonomy with his record company—RCA, for which he had turned out ten successful records since 1961—and agreed to make the recording happen.

Bley rewrote most of the compositions she intended to use so that they would accommodate Burton's quartet (which included Swallow, the guitarist Larry Coryell, and the drummer Bob Moses) and an additional sextet (whose members played trumpet; trombone; bass trombone; soprano, tenor, and baritone saxophones; and tuba). During the summer of 1967 Bley and the sextet players spent some time in Sausalito, California, where Burton's quartet had a summer engagement at a venue called the Trident, run by an assistant to the Village Vanguard's founder, Max Gordon. They also played a series of nights at the Fillmore, across the bay in San Francisco. They shared the bill with the British rock band Cream, thus providing an initial encounter between Carla Bley and Cream's bassist and singer, Jack Bruce, with whom she would collaborate extensively in the future (as would Mantler, who was a member of the sextet).[4] When the Burton quartet was not performing, the players rehearsed Bley's compositions on a rented houseboat in Sausalito. The group's New York studio time in late 1967 and early 1968 resulted in an unusual album of both lyricism and power called *A Genuine Tong Funeral*. Bley titled the work for a scene from a French movie depicting a funeral procession in Hong Kong. In connection with the funereal motif, she described her piece as "a dark opera without words." As prearranged with RCA, the recording was released under Burton's name, though Bley had composed and orchestrated all the music, led the recording sessions, played the piano part, and conducted the ensemble. (Shortly thereafter, a version of *A Genuine Tong Funeral* without Bley's involvement was filmed for the final episode of *Mixed Bag* on Boston's public television station, WGBH.) The twenty-five-year-old Burton, who had taken a considerable professional risk by recording Bley's experimental "concept album" on the mainstream label that had supported him for nearly a decade, was named the youngest ever "Jazzman of the Year" by *Down Beat* in 1968; the same magazine gave *A Genuine Tong Funeral* five stars.

Bley had composed *The Survivors* and *The New National Anthem*, the first pieces that would become a part of *A Genuine Tong Funeral*, as early as 1964. In 1966, at Steve Swallow's request, she wrote *Silent Spring*, which would become one of the central extended sections of *A Genuine Tong Funeral*.[5] The remaining pieces were written in 1967 specifically for Burton after he became interested in the original collection; the vibraphonist had already recorded Bley's *Mother of the Dead Man* prior to its inclusion in *A Genuine Tong Funeral*. Burton recalls: "I loved the compositional strength of her writing, and found her to be fascinatingly eccentric."[6] Her conception of the work was indeed far-reaching, if not quite fully "eccentric": in an introduction to the piece Bley wrote that she thought of *A Genuine Tong Funeral* as a dramatic work that should be at least partially staged, including lighting effects and costumes for the musicians, an intent likely influenced by the theatrics of the psychedelic rock movement. According to Bley, the thematic thread running through this "dark opera without words"—one reflected by many of the individual composition titles, such as *Some Dirge, Mother of the Dead Man, Grave Train, The New Funeral March, The Survivors*, and so on—explored "emotions toward death, from the most irreverent to those of deepest loss."

Essentially a programmatic chamber suite with refrains, thematic development, and formal coherence, *A Genuine Tong Funeral* is made up of ten individual pieces, one of which, *Morning* (not *Mourning*), is repeated as a variation. The suite has a dramatic curve that covers a wide emotional range, from the previously mentioned irreverence to deep loss. These emotions are expressed through various instrumental combinations, densities, and textures. The unusual instrumental forces provided Bley a wider yet well-defined sonic palette, and with these added resources she synthesized attention-grabbing new orchestral colors. The orchestra resulted from the combination of the two separate forces already mentioned: the Gary Burton Quartet and an all-star sextet that included two reed players (Gato Barbieri and Steve Lacy), three brass players (Howard Johnson, Jimmy Knepper, and Michael Mantler), and Bley herself on piano and organ. Some of the individual pieces in *A Genuine Tong Funeral*, such as *The New Funeral March*, were originally conceived for the sextet alone and are available as an arranged score; *The New Funeral March* published score is notable for its "explanation of the notation," in which Bley writes that "the length of the lines and spaces are accurate if the eye moves at a steady speed across the page; there is time within the phrases but no overall steady tempo."

Throughout the work Bley varies the instrumental combinations, allowing individuals to speak in their most articulate and eloquent voices. Nonetheless, much of the music was completely written out. This feature makes this work something of an anomaly for the time and may have affected its reception, especially in certain circles in Western Europe, where free jazz had become the dominant dogma of the day. Several sections, such as the more traditional jazz tune *Intermission Music*, highlight the quartet alone; others place the brass and reed crowd in the shadows, acting as keeners at a burial, relentlessly repeating the same pitch, riff, or rhythm, while some other lone mourner laments, wails, or screams in pain. The frequent tonal stasis and reliance on ostinato patterns provides accompaniments with minimal restrictions for the freer solo sections. Regarding this kind of texture in later big-band arrangements, Roswell Rudd recalls: "I can remember her cueing these backgrounds, these things happening behind the solos. I remember her where she would start something, or cut it off, or fade it out, or start something else—there might be several of these episodes during a solo, changing the texture in real time. She might nudge the soloist. I remember getting more than one of these nudges."[7]

Though Bley had been writing and arranging for nearly a decade, *A Genuine Tong Funeral* was her first extended project, beyond *Roast*, in composing for specific players. Some pieces display Bley's masterful orchestrations of completely written-out and conducted material, while others, such as *Intermission Music*, function more as traditional jazz tunes, providing a base for improvisation by an independent small ensemble. This piece is a tuneful waltz, and in *A Genuine Tong Funeral* it serves as a vehicle for Burton and his quartet to improvise without the constraints of written-out parts. The tonality of the piece is ambiguous (Bley herself has said that she printed the piece without chord symbols—typically written for players who don't read traditional notation well—because many of them were too complicated to figure out), though much of it hovers around C-sharp, and it ends on what seems to be C-sharp major. This loose chromatic ramble maintains the triple feel of a waltz throughout—except near the beginning, when it slips into 2/4. (Dmitri Shostakovich uses a similar stumbling effect in his Preludes, op. 34, no. 17, also a waltz.) The thin, dancelike texture and its generally predictable rhythmic patterns (if not tonal ones) might be taken as demonstrations of Bley's insistence during this period on making things "simple and plain." At the same time, the work contains an emotional quality she attributes to Albert Ayler, whose music, she claims, gave her permission to be "maudlin."[8]

Discussions of Bley as an orchestrator and a band leader often lead to comparisons with Ellington and Mingus because of her ability to write for individual players and not for their generic instruments and her refusal to allow them merely to blend into the band. Mantler explained his view of her practice: "She usually writes specifically for particular musicians, thereby allowing them to add their own personalities within her compositional frameworks."[9] Likewise, *Intermission Music* and *Mother of the Dead Man* allowed Burton to shine as lead soloist, and *Grave Train* spotlights his quartet, but he and his band by no means dominate the recording. Different players are foregrounded in different pieces—for example, Lacy in *Fanfare*, Barbieri in *Silent Spring*, Knepper and Coryell in *Some Dirge*, and Mantler in *The New Funeral March*. The composer highlights her own role at the piano in a very poignant way near the end of the entire piece.

A Genuine Tong Funeral's success as a large composition stems in part from its overarching structure. The resulting architecture is classically balanced, with a fairly symmetrical form in terms of the proportions and placement of the pieces. Bley insists that any such large-scale design was purely an accident. Nonetheless, the first piece and the last piece are almost exactly the same length, and both contain the same fanfare figure; this figure is first heard two minutes into the piece, and it serves as an abrupt but light-hearted (not to mention mischievous) coda. Likewise, the second and ninth pieces are similar in length and character. Both feature tremolos on the low notes of the piano and achieve a sense of stopping time. The second piece, *Death Rolls*, takes its title literally, consisting only of static drum and piano rolls, a programmatic depiction of something somber, severe, and dark. Working inward, the third and eighth pieces are *Morning, part 1*, and *Morning, part 2*, variations on the same music that take up approximately the same length of time. Here, too, Bley includes a declamatory, static, three-note fanfare motive, embellished whimsically with ascending and descending slides; perhaps the trombone slides are meant to remind the listener of marching funeral bands in New Orleans. The *Morning* pair also includes a dotted ostinato rhythmic pattern that makes an appearance in the sixth piece as well. Also, several pieces end ominously with a lone low bass note on the piano. These instances of material repeated throughout the piece help orient the listener's ear to certain musical characters at the "funeral." The fourth piece, *Intermission Music*, provides the most traditional jazz in *A Genuine Tong Funeral*. The dramatic weight of the suite is provided by the two longest numbers: the fifth piece, *Silent Spring*, and the seventh, *Some Dirge*. Both running some eight minutes long, these pieces throw the album's structure slightly off balance from its otherwise nearly symmetrical axis, a welcome disruption that seems to provide the emotional climax of the moody yet extroverted work.

The opening and closing pieces of *A Genuine Tong Funeral* provide great stylistic contrast while simultaneously supporting a sense of proportional balance to the composition as a whole. The first piece, a small suite-within-a-suite, consists of several sections titled *The Opening, Shovels, The Survivors*, and *Grave*

Train. The Opening is a slow, smooth, tonal brass chorale reminiscent of the opening of the Largo from Dvořák's Ninth ("New World") Symphony (a piece Bley later orchestrated for the eighteen-piece Liberation Music Orchestra on their fourth release, *Not in Our Name* [2005]). *The Opening* appears to be completely written out and conducted, with trombone slides articulating points of rest. Burton enters on vibes, and a short improvisatory section follows (presumably the section titled *Shovels*). *The Survivors* appears as the first fanfare figure, the same one that ends the piece. When it recurs at the end of the entire work, this music is again identified as *The Survivors*, drawing attention to the cyclic nature of the work as a whole and perhaps suggesting that "survivors" sometimes celebrate in the face of death, most notably at wakes. The section that follows *The Survivors*, called *Grave Train*, sounds much like a Kurt Weill tune. Bley has said it is not an arrangement of Weill, though she did attend a performance of Brecht and Weill's *Threepenny Opera* in New York around this time and was excited and influenced by the sound of that music. At the end of *Grave Train*, the orchestra suddenly falls silent, and we briefly hear the terrifying sound of heavy chains. Other than this startling sound effect, *Grave Train* is upbeat and playful, tonal and rhythmic. Stylistically it unambiguously references the not-so-distant world of musical theater, where dramatic power and accessibility are acceptable artistic goals.

By contrast, the final piece of *A Genuine Tong Funeral*, called *The New National Anthem*, enters an entirely different world: the tangled, anarchic, searching world of free improvisation during the mid- to late 1960s. The central section of this closing number is initiated by the quartet playing very fast, angular, seemingly unorganized and uncoordinated material; gradually the other players enter with similar phrases. The texture becomes very dense and chaotic, until all ten players seem to be engaging with the aggressive, self-serious "high energy hateful screaming music" with which Bley had become so frustrated during her European tour with Brötzmann and Kowald. Gradually the players drop out, the texture thins, and at the moment when the last one has departed from the sonic landscape, Bley emerges from the background with a series of thick and emphatic piano chords anchored by a repeated low pedal note. This sudden and unexpected surfacing of the piano as a distinctive voice after nearly forty-five minutes of ensemble music—during which the piano is rarely featured—gives the impression of the mysteriously hidden composer stepping out from behind a tree at the funeral. We realize she was there all along, and she is the most important guest.

The stylistic contrast evident through this brief comparison of the transparent, light-hearted Weill-like section of the opening and the opaque, intense, free-jazz section of the close nicely indicates the kind of emotional range of which

Bley was capable and demonstrates how her assimilation and synthesis of different musical styles helped guide her exploration of larger structures. In addition, the framing of the work may allude to *Sergeant Pepper's Lonely Hearts Club Band*, an acknowledged model and inspiration for *A Genuine Tong Funeral*. The Beatles' concept album provided a similar emotional contrast between the happy-go-lucky second song "A Little Help from My Friends" and the dark, experimental closing, "A Day in the Life." Bley's work is the cultural product of a time when many musicians were heavily influenced by new developments in soul, rhythm and blues, and rock, and by the Beatles in particular, especially the compositional and conceptual innovations and the unprecedented stylistic eclecticism of *Sergeant Pepper's*. Eager to move away from the miniature forms she had written in the past, Bley took *Sergeant Pepper's* as an open invitation to venture into something more grandiose—program music, and the high expressivity typical of romanticism. *A Genuine Tong Funeral* is an ambitious tone poem disguised as an entertaining jazz record. After all, Bley claimed, the Beatles constituted "the next important change in [her] life after Ornette."[10] Bley's first fully realized, scored, and structured work demonstrated without a doubt her ability to maintain creative control over a wide variety of musical materials, musicians, and the recording process itself. All these skills would serve her well in her next large-form project, *Escalator over the Hill*.

5 | *Escalator over the Hill*

Jazz Opera as Fusion

It just all went together for me; it was like being an actor in a troupe, whenever I got in the same room with these great improvisers, these great personalities. People will say to me, "You were on the cusp of the civil rights protest," and that turmoil was going on, and it was in all of us, and it was all in the music. It's hard to separate it out for me because it just goes together. And the beauty of it was to get all of that diversified energy into one room at the same time and see what would happen. Because that was the barometer. That was the atmosphere of the time. That was the acoustic atmosphere. That was what we were trying to get, and that was basic to what we were doing.

—Roswell Rudd

BLEY HAD BEEN WORKING on a piece she called *Detective Writer Daughter* when the poet Paul Haines (1932–2003) sent her a set of original surrealist poems that seemed to fit with her music.[1] This poetry would serve as the foundation for her most ambitious work to date: *Escalator over the Hill*. As a child Bley had worked on a collection of songs called *Over the Hill*, but she insists this early work had no relation to *Escalator over the Hill* beyond a coincidental title. She had never set words to music before, at least not since she was a child, and she was not particularly interested in what the words might mean from a narrative point of view.

At some point during the creation of *Escalator over the Hill*, Mantler and Bley moved to a farm near Bangor, Maine, where Bley had bought one hundred acres of land with a $1,300 commission she had earned orchestrating Charlie Haden's first Liberation Music Orchestra record. Much of the recording of *Escalator over the Hill*, however, took place in New York City, largely at Joseph Papp's Public Theater, and elsewhere in the country—and in other countries for parts of some tracks. The production of *Escalator over the Hill* as a recording was logistically complicated by the fact that the dozens of musicians she used were scattered over the world and frequently traveling. Eventually they recorded in the RCA studios with Ray Hall, an engineer with whom Bley had enjoyed working while recording *A Genuine Tong Funeral*. Bley has documented the staggeringly confusing details of the production process in an account that was originally published in *Impetus* magazine in 1976.

Though the work is colloquially referred to as a "jazz opera," its creators called it a "chronotransduction," a term coined by Sheridan ("Sherry") Speeth, a scientist who was friends with Haines. After moving to India, Speeth would donate some $15,000 to the recording project; another friend helped secure a $30,000 loan from a bank. These loans and donations were critical to the survival of the project, for commercial record companies took no interest in Bley's conception of the work. Haines himself organized an unsuccessful fundraiser in Washington, D.C., while Bley wrote to Yoko Ono, Pete Townshend, and other rich and famous people asking them to support the project financially. In most cases she received no reply. In the meantime, Bley and Mantler continued their work with the Jazz Composers Orchestra, including several extremely long performances—lasting some six hours—during April 1969 at the Electric Circus, the East Village nightclub made famous by Andy Warhol and the Velvet Underground. Bley embarked almost simultaneously on her first large-scale collaboration with Charlie Haden and his Liberation Music Orchestra, which rehearsed in Ornette Coleman's Soho loft on Prince Street. In 1971, around the time the recording and mixing processes for *Escalator over the Hill* were finally complete, Bley won her second *Down Beat* International Critics Poll award as a composer.

Widely considered Bley's greatest achievement, as well as Paul Haines's most consequential piece of poetic writing, the musically unclassifiable *Escalator over the Hill* is an epic, somewhat impenetrable work of art, one that nourished Bley's proclivity toward musical boundary crossing and her genuinely collaborative nature. It was the first record released in her own name, and every aspect of this production (aside from the poetry) belonged to Bley, from composing, arranging, playing, singing, and conducting to editing and mixing the tapes and preparing the master. Far surpassing her own concept album ambitions demonstrated in *A Genuine Tong Funeral*, all dimensions of *Escalator over the Hill* are extravagant. The long (a triple album, nearly two hours), stylistically eclectic work fuses singers and players from all over the musical map—fifty-three individuals participated in the recording, including some of the most productive and original jazz and rock musicians working at the time: Gato Barbieri, Karl Berger, Jack Bruce, Don Cherry, Charlie Haden, Leroy Jenkins, Paul Jones, Sheila Jordan, Jeanne Lee, Michael Mantler, John McLaughlin, Paul Motian, Don Preston, and Roswell Rudd. One reviewer called this "complex infrastructure" a "combination of vocal and orchestral music, opera, song cycle, oratorio, and musical comedy."[2] From the start, Bley imagined an eventual film version of the piece. The work as a whole seems simultaneously to assimilate and annihilate rock gestures, jazz harmonies, and classical structures. By nature of its absolute autonomy, *Escalator over the Hill* also seems to thumb its nose at all musical authorities and institutions, particularly the recording industry. In this sense it is perhaps *the* quintessential antiestablishment statement of its time.[3]

Haines's poetry, sent to Bley from his home in India, provided a loose libretto on which she developed an instrumental strategy for designing contrasting musical entities. The libretto cryptically introduces characters who live in "Cecil Clark's hotel" in Rawalpindi, Pakistan, and include the expatriates Ginger (sung by Linda Ronstadt) and Jack (sung by Jack Bruce), as well as some twenty other figures with bizarre monikers, such as "Ancient Roomer," "Used Woman," "Yodeling Ventriloquist," and "Sand Shepherd" (played by Don Cherry); she originally had hoped that the singer-songwriter Randy Newman would become involved as one of the featured performers. Bley gave herself the roles of "Leader, Mutant, Voice, Desert Woman." These solo characters are complemented by an additional collection of "Phantoms, Multiple Public Members, Hotelpeople, Women, Men, Flies, Bullfrogs, Mindsweepers, Speakers, Blindman." These parts were largely played by the principal soloists, who included—in addition to Bley, Bruce, Cherry, and Ronstadt—Charlie Haden, Sheila Jordan, Jeanne Lee, Paul Jones, Karen Mantler, Don Preston, Perry Robinson, Roswell Rudd, Viva, and the president of JCOA, Timothy Marquand, as "Therapist." (As was the case with Stockhausen's theatrical *Originale*, which Bley had seen performed in Cologne in 1961, many of the performers in some sense played themselves.) Steve Gebhardt, who made a film that documents the elaborate recording process of *Escalator over the Hill*, was recruited as an extra. The beautifully photographed and edited film by Gebhardt provides rare documentation of the intricate process of rehearsing and recording the many layers of this enormous work. It reveals a confident yet relaxed Bley as a patient, generous, and precise leader (even when telling her musicians to ignore the written music and do whatever they like), as well as a very physical player and conductor and a surprisingly courageous vocalist. Her energy, abandon, and obvious clarity about her goals in these sessions elicited astoundingly strong vocal and instrumental performances from all involved, despite the difficulty of the music.

From an instrumental point of view, *Escalator over the Hill* is essentially a Jazz Composers Orchestra project, and Bley wrote parts specifically for many of her favorite players: Barbieri, Cherry, Haden, Mantler, Rudd, and other virtuosic improvisers are often given the spotlight for extended solos, though they are also easily absorbed into the fabric of the whole. In addition to providing these solo highlights, Bley organized the twenty-four musicians into five distinct ensembles: (1) "Orchestra (and Hotel Lobby Band)," a nineteen-piece big band that included, aside from the usual reeds, brass, and rhythm section, two French horns, viola, vibraphone, congas, orchestral bells, and celesta; (2) the "Original Hotel Amateur Band" (a name that might refer to the Original Dixieland Jazz Band), a nine-piece band including the artist-filmmaker Michael Snow on trumpet; (3) the "Desert Band," an eight-piece group playing Middle Eastern–inflected music, dominated by Cherry's microtonal trumpet playing and supported by Leroy Jenkins on violin and Paul Motian on doumbek; (4) "Jack's Traveling Band," a standard rock configuration of organ, guitar, bass, and drums that highlighted the singing of Jack Bruce; and (5) "Phantom Music," a trio producing a variety of otherworldly sound effects with the help of organ, celesta, chimes, calliope, prepared piano, and a Moog synthesizer.[4] Bley played in all five ensembles and also conducted the larger ones.

The elaborate instrumentation of *Escalator over the Hill* reflects Bley's eclectic tastes, as well as the serendipity and haphazardness of her casting; having little money to pay performers, Bley notoriously drew in everyone she could, plus their relatives and roommates. The musical casting also expressed her affinity for rock music, low brass, elaborate orchestral color, ecstatic solos, and occasional experimentation with electronics and unusual sound effects. The Orchestra/Hotel Lobby Band sets the stage with the opera's overture, which not surprisingly introduces major themes that recur later. This ensemble was made up of expert and experienced players (and was so large that it had to rehearse in the old Cinematheque space, which Jonas Mekas graciously made available). The Original Hotel Amateur Band provides a foil to this group of professionals and points to something Bley would come to explore frequently in her music after this point, what one might affectionately term "imperfection."[5] In *Escalator over the Hill* this quality is manifested in the "amateur" band, which included not only actual amateurs but also skilled musicians playing unfamiliar instruments. For example, in playing valve trombone, Mantler was one of "four regular musicians who were good enough to play amateurishly as a favor," as Bley put it.

Another aspect of Bley's fascination with imperfection was expressed through the use of untrained singers, as well as a manner of nonmelodic speech-singing reminiscent perhaps of Harry Partch's "intoning voice," Robert Ashley's singsong narrations, or even Arnold Schoenberg's early twentieth-century technique of *Sprechstimme*.[6] In *Escalator over the Hill* Bley enlisted her young daughter, Karen, as well as the "Warhol Superstar" and actress Viva and a host of other nonsingers, many of whom were also nonmusician friends. Several years after completing *Escalator over the Hill*, Bley would further explore the expressive possibilities of imperfection to great dramatic and comic effect (e.g., Roswell Rudd's narration in *Musique Mecanique part 2* [1978] and the drummer D. Sharpe's singing in *I Hate to Sing* [1983]). These explorations moved Bley further away from the virtuosity that had served as a foundation for instrumental jazz in the past and aligned her in many ways with several avant-garde groups of the late 1960s and early 1970s—Musica Elettronica Viva, the Scratch Orchestra, and the Portsmouth Sinfonia, to name just a few—many of which explored group improvisation and unconventional performance practices to distance themselves from the elitist implications of virtuosity, complexity, and the exclusion-based hierarchy of most established classical musical networks and institutions. Similarly, though avant-garde jazz musicians did not tend to work with amateurs, Bley's varied settings of Haines's poetry also aligned her with their trend of using theatric recitations of text during the late 1960s. The New York Art Quartet and the Art Ensemble of Chicago are just two of many groups that explored the creative and performative connections between poetry and improvisation during this time.

In this regard, Haines's poetry provided an ideal vehicle for Bley's exploration of the voice. Of his contribution to the music of the time, Haines's close friend Roswell Rudd said: "His instrument was words. I've always considered him a jazz musician, an improviser. And it just comes out as words with him. But he's one of the great jazz soloists."[7] Haines's deep connection to live jazz since the late 1940s—in Chicago, Detroit, New Orleans, New York City, and elsewhere—appears on the surface of his writings, which during the 1960s included liner notes and other contributions to Paul Bley's *Footloose*, Albert Ayler's *Spiritual Unity*, the Jazz Composers Orchestra's *Communication*, and the first recording (the only one prior to *Escalator over the Hill*) on the Jazz Composers Orchestra Association label. He continued writing about avant-garde and improvised music during the decades to follow. He also recorded the first performance that the Jazz Composers Orchestra gave in the dance studio above the Village Vanguard and, as was mentioned earlier, served as a recording engineer for Michael Snow's film score to *New York Eye and Ear Control*. Snow recalled Haines as being "totally music-centered."[8] Though he is perhaps most closely associated with Carla Bley because of the massive proportions and legendary status of *Escalator over the Hill*, Haines was close to and collaborated with a wide variety of other composers and musicians throughout his life. Stuart Broomer, who edited a collection of Haines's work, states that his writing "possesses many of the qualities of his favorite players: the breadth of wit and the sentiment of Roswell Rudd, the understatement of Paul Bley or John Tchicai, or the harmonic subtlety of Carla Bley, with its constant sense of doubleness and dislocation. That sense of dislocation is true of many of those to whom he listens most closely, from Professor Longhair to Warne Marsh to Derek Bailey."[9]

Strangely colloquial and surreal at the same time, Haines's poetry permits subjective interpretation at best. Some of it has a "Lucy in the Sky with Diamonds" psychedelic flavor: "Parrots so green they make your eyes seem blue," sings Jack Bruce in *Rawalpindi Blues*, in connection to nothing in particular. Similarly, the following passage is sung by the character of Cecil Clark in the titular section near the beginning of the opera:

PEOPLE WHO NEVER
TELL ANYONE ANYTHING
ALWAYS
JUST LETTING THEM KNOW
FLOODING MEMORY WITH PUMPS
TALENTED TEAMS OF ONIONS
INSIDE THE GOAL
OF THE MOUTH
ITSELF.

Some passages seem like exercises in wordplay of the sort that Bley cultivated in many of her composition titles. This passage is sung by Jack Bruce "in the music hall" in a section called "Businessmen":

BUSINESSMEN DEEPLY AWAKE
SLEEPING LIKE SPINNING TOPS
CORNER THE SMALLTOWN
MASTOID MARKET
THEIR UVULAS HOPPING MAD
BENEATH BONEY EARACHE PROFITS
PUNISHED BY BEING KEPT ALIVE
SURE OF THE PAST AT LAST
ALWAYS A LITTLE SORRY
ABOUT REALITY.

In one of the opera's most memorable songs, "Why," Linda Ronstadt evokes a different profession:

NURSES DYING THEIR HAIR
DON'T CARE
IF THE HORSE IS LOCKED
THE HOUSE STILL THERE.
IT DOESN'T SEEM
TO MATTER TO THEM
THE TRACES
OF HORSES
AND PINEAPPLE
AND CHEESE
SO MANY INGREDIENTS
IN THE SOUP . . .

To this Charlie Haden answers in a Midwestern drawl: "NO ROOM FOR A SPOON!"

An intriguing aspect of the physical product of the recording, evident only by reading the "libretto" included with the vinyls, is that some of Haines's poetry is printed but not actually heard. The script includes this "silent" poetry within sections where instrumental music alone occurs. For example, in the instrumental section labeled "Hotel Lobby Band," near the beginning of the opera, the following phrases are printed but neither spoken nor sung:

DIRECT PULSE
PASSES BY
DARTS IN LIMITING
THE SYSTEM
ALL GREEN WITHIN
ALL PALE WITH GO
A WHISTLING ECHO
ALL FOR FUN
FROM SINCLAIR'S
BLUE MAGIC GUN.

Later, during the Hotel Lobby Band's instrumental rendition of "Holiday in Risk Theme," this musing appears:

IF I BELIEVE I AM YOU
(SINCE I DO)
WHO IS WRONG
AGAIN?
NOT THAT THAT

MIGHT BE THE SAME
(FOR THAT MIGHT BE)
BUT NOT THAT THAT.

Parsing such abstruse philosophy is perhaps beside the point of appreciating *Escalator over the Hill*, which might be better celebrated as a three-ring circus of conceptual art, poetry, and elaborate musical designs in the form of a dramatic yet unstaged spectacle. In the end, this "chronotransduction" is more akin to oratorio than opera.

The connections among words, poetry, lyrics, melody, and voices constitutes a dominant and ongoing theme in Bley's work. Until she was about thirty-three years old, she seems to have set no text except in her song *Jesus Maria*, published in a collection of Christmas carols she arranged for piano and guitar. With *Escalator over the Hill*, she started exploring the connections in unique and fruitful ways. In an interview later in her career, she told Ben Sidran that for a few years she used a technique she referred to as the "Fantasy World," in which she would think of verbal phrases that would lead her to certain melodies. Bley did not use these English sentences as lyrics, however, and the melodies based on them would eventually start to imply their own continuations, harmonies, and orchestrations. This verbal approach to musical composition might further explain the strength and originality of Bley's themes.

In addition to juxtaposing amateurs and professionals, Bley conceptualized the relationship between the Desert Band and Jack's Traveling Band as a sort of dialogue between East and West, and indeed, that cultural confrontation serves as a musical and thematic subtext throughout *Escalator over the Hill*. The first recording sessions, in late November and early December 1970, were devoted to the climactic and cathartic song *Rawalpindi Blues*, which offers a sonic synthesis of disparate forces. Just as Bley wrote many of the instrumental parts for specific musical personalities (in particular, Barbieri, Cherry, McLaughlin, and Rudd), she wrote much of *Escalator over the Hill* with Jack Bruce in mind. The song *Rawalpindi Blues* is an effective vehicle for Bruce's hot, dynamic, tight-jeaned vocal style, and his singing adds breathless urgency and tension to this far from relaxed "blues." Only the introduction is relaxed, opening with a slow, meandering reference to the main motive of Bley's early piece *Vashkar*. But *Rawalpindi Blues* soon becomes an extended rock jam session with John McLaughlin. The music in this section has little if any connection to traditional jazz. Instead, it reflects an art-rock sensibility much in the air at the time. Bley seems to possess an uncanny knack for unlocking her players' strongest abilities; in *Escalator over the Hill* she gave Bruce difficult and expressive vocal lines that showcased his talents as a singer.

The logistical challenges of *Escalator over the Hill* were substantial, partly because many of Bley's key performers were touring or had home bases in different countries. For their "Jack and Ginger" duets, for example, Bruce and Ronstadt recorded separately in London and Los Angeles, and the tracks were mixed later. Likewise, Charlie Haden claimed, "I didn't meet Linda Ronstadt but I sang a duet with her."[10] Like much of Bley's work, *Escalator over the Hill* favors heterophony (simultaneous but not synchronous playing of the same melodies) and contrapuntal layering. Here the layering occurs not only in the instrumental and vocal writing but in the technology itself. Bley, working with the RCA recording engineer Ray Hall, described the complicated process of mixing the sixteen-track tapes they had made for *Rawalpindi Blues* as one of the most unnerving and time-consuming parts of the entire project. This elaborate attention to sonic layering is part of what makes the work as a whole so rich.

For all its density, complexity, virtuosity, and whimsy, *Escalator over the Hill* also thematically connects the beginning and the end, creating a symmetrical unity much like that in *A Genuine Tong Funeral*. This theme concerns the concept of reincarnation—connecting also to the idea of "chronotransduction"—and the concept of the eternal return of the same. This is expressed during lengthy sections near the opening and close of the piece by Bruce's repeatedly sung phrase "It's Again"—perhaps a reference to his 1967 performance of the Cream song "As You Said," during which he sings the word *again* over and over—and by the extended unison drone, a D hummed by Bley and several members of the ensemble and multi-layered in the editing process, that ends *Escalator over the Hill*. In pressing the vinyl itself, the technician "locked the groove on the final hum in order to make it seem to go on forever." (This effect is lessened with the CD reissue, on which the final drone lasts only about eighteen minutes.)

More than some of her other works, which might be designated "Third Stream" (i.e., blending classical idioms with jazz idioms), *Escalator over the Hill* is more readily classifiable as "fusion," namely, a blend of improvised jazz and electrified rock. Yet it also defies classification because of its inclusion of snippets of country music, operatic singing, non-Western melodies, electronic soundscapes, and Ronstadt's pop singer pathos. This "jazz opera" looks back to similarly unprecedented adventurous spectacles such as Harry Partch's multimedia works and looks forward to Frank Zappa's unperformable, unstaged, spoken (not sung), and largely conceptual "opera pantomime" called *Civilization Phaze III*.

In 1972, after Bley had spent nearly five years continuously managing complicated musical and practical matters, *Escalator over the Hill* was released as a triple album in opulent packaging as JCOA 2.[11] Though it was certainly overshadowed by the 1970 Columbia Records release of Miles Davis's landmark studio double album *Bitches Brew*, which established an authoritative context for the style of fusion, the critical reception of *Escalator over the Hill* was surprisingly widespread (despite its being released on a tiny independent label)—reviews appeared even in the *Omaha World Herald* and *Penthouse*—and overwhelmingly positive. (One reviewer wrote: "Imagine all the musical audacity of *Sergeant Pepper* with better performers, a totally abstract libretto, and three times the length," while another called Bley and Mantler "two of the most respected composers in the field of new music.")[12] In 1972 Bley received a Guggenheim grant for composition. By June of that year, according to Mantler, about five thousand copies of *Escalator over the Hill* had already been sold.

6 | *Copyright Royalties*

New Music
Distribution Service

AROUND 1970 THE INTERRELATED ENSEMBLE casts of the Jazz Composers Orchestra, the Liberation Music Orchestra, and *Escalator over the Hill* constituted a growing network of independent and innovative composer-performers. On the release of *Escalator over the Hill* in March 1972, Bley and Mantler started a new division of the Jazz Composers Orchestra Association, a nonprofit organization called the New Music Distribution Service (NMDS). The NMDS was designed to provide a "desperately needed alternative to the music industry machine," according to a JCOA publicity flyer. The NMDS, which showed "strong signs of health after a shaky start," constituted a musician-run service "for the distribution of all independently produced recordings of new music regardless of commercial potential or personal use."[1] The purpose of the NMDS harked back to the ideals of the Jazz Composers Guild, though without the laborious union-like decision-making process. It aimed, namely, to give musicians total artistic and economic control over their recorded work. Although the service itself was supported by the New York State Council for the Arts, the National Endowment for the Arts, "other concerned individuals," and later the Ford and Mobil Foundations, it maintained administrative autonomy. The NMDS catalog explicitly promoted the noncommercial, less-popular strains of jazz, classical, and rock music, doing so perhaps for the first time anywhere, especially en masse, and creating a space where these experimental traditions could exist side by side and interact—a "networking resource," in the words of Gregory Tate, who contributed a foreword for the 1986 catalog.

Though its name includes a stylistic genre, the Jazz Composers Orchestra Association focused on the creation of avant-garde compositions of many types; acting in this spirit, the NMDS focused on new music in a broad sense, with inclusiveness at its core: "We wanted to let a thousand flowers bloom," as Timothy Marquand put it.[2] This diverse array reflected Bley's growing identification with a wider variety of musical styles and her ongoing exploration of jazz's position with regard to both mass-marketed popular music and the niche genres of the classical avant-garde. Much like the immediate model of *Escalator over the Hill* itself, all the "new music" referenced in the NMDS's name emerged from the minds of composers who insisted on economic independence and artistic freedom. Moreover, this music could not be easily categorized. Interestingly, however, the NMDS came up with its own categories for selling "package deals" in the following areas: "New Music Classics" (e.g., John Cage, Henry Cowell, Harry Partch, and Edgard Varèse), "Contemporary New Music" (e.g., Lou Harrison, Daniel Lentz, and Pauline Oliveros), "Electronic Music" (e.g., Alvin Lucier and Gordon Mumma), "New Jazz" (e.g., Bley, Anthony Braxton, Cecil Taylor, and Henry Threadgill), and "Experimental Music" (e.g., Robert Ashley, Rhys Chatham, Fred Frith, and Henry Kaiser).

Bley recalls trying to interest jazz-oriented record producers in her work around this time, contacting Teo Macero at Columbia Records, Nesuhi Ertegun at Atlantic Records, and Francis Wolff at Blue Note Records with no success.[3] Yet she was buoyed by the critical acclaim that *Escalator over the Hill* had earned within a year of its release: it won the French Grand Prix du Disque du Jazz in 1973 and was named LP of the year in the 1973 jazz poll by the British magazine *Melody Maker*; in addition, *Down Beat* had named Bley a "Talent Deserving of Wider Recognition" for three years in a row.

In May 1973 Bley and Mantler decided to found their own record label. They called it Watt Works. Watt constituted a further commitment to the DIY attitude Bley and her colleagues had cultivated since the days of the "October Revolution in Jazz" and demonstrated the belief that taking matters into one's own hands is as much a political-economic act as it is a musical-artistic one. The New Music Distribution Service provided a means of disseminating JCOA and Watt products, along with everything else in the growing network's catalog. After Bley and Mantler began selling more records of their own, they moved the distribution of JCOA and Watt products out of NMDS: first, briefly, to Virgin Records and then to ECM so as to not overtax the resources of their small distribution service and to allow their own music to be distributed more broadly.

The first release on the new Watt label was Bley's record *Tropical Appetites*. Affectionately considered a little sister to *Escalator over the Hill*, it too made use of poetry by Paul Haines, and this collection of songs also was planned as something like a concept album. Perhaps the most memorable of these settings is *The Funnybird Song*, which includes Bley's then six-year-old daughter, Karen, and the gruffly charming Mothers of Invention keyboardist Don Preston on vocals. This song is just over a minute long, but it is captivating in its sweetness and simple beauty. It shows Bley's gift for songwriting as well as her skill at setting unconventional voices. The melody is conventional, tuneful, and easy to sing and to remember. The instrumentation is whimsical, with something like a breathy calliope coming in during the second verse. (Bley later included an instrumental version of this song, with a wonderful tuba solo by Bob Stewart, on her album *Dinner Music* [1977]). Over the next few years, several JCOA albums were released on Watt as well, including recordings of large works by Don Cherry, Clifford Thornton, and Grachan Moncur III. The network of activity guided by the Bley-Mantler partnership had grown into something like a grassroots recording and distribution conglomerate.

According to Bley's own estimate, the NMDS initially carried about thirty labels (though by 1984, she reported, this number had risen to 350). These early labels included Bley and Mantler's Watt, Manfred Eicher's Munich-based label ECM, Black Saint, Free Music Production, Opus One, and CRI, among others. The NMDS—which continually emphasized that it was a service, not a business— became critically important for soon-to-be-successful artists working in a wide variety of musical styles: Laurie Anderson (performance art), Chick Corea (jazz fusion), Gil-Scott Heron (jazz poetry/soul), John Zorn ("downtown" improvisation), and many others for whom the NMDS distributed independently produced recordings early in their careers. This category included works on Philip Glass's Chatham Square label, established in 1971, through which he released his influential minimalist tours-de-force *Music with Changing Parts* (1971), *Music in Fifths* (1973), and *Music in Similar Motion* (1973). Though much of the music they distributed would go on to enjoy popularity and international influence, Bley and Mantler made a point of being completely nondirective in their choices about the material they distributed. They refused to make value judgments based on aesthetic preferences or expectations. If something gained too much popularity, however, they had to drop it from the catalog. Such was the case with high-volume sellers by Chick Corea and Gil-Scott Heron.

Beyond playing a role in connecting the strands of an underground and independent international musical network, the NMDS constituted yet another creative outlet for Bley, who used its occasional newsletters and catalogs (as well as other Watt publications, such as *The Watt Works Family* [1990] and *The Watt Family Scrapbook* [1994]) to express both her sense of humor and her serious concerns regarding the myriad quagmires facing composers in the United States. She also celebrated their resilience and their diversity. The winter 1974 NMDS newsletter, for instance, announced that it disseminated "news from and about idealists, strays, upstarts, innovators, crusaders, visionaries, rejects, bulwarks, perfectionists, seekers, over-achievers, unknowns, radicals, optimists, anarchists, dropouts, and geniuses." It also included an astounding list of the over 230 musicians who had played with the Jazz Composers Orchestra by that time.

Most important, the winter 1974 issue printed an informative article by Bley called "Friendly Independent Record Makers." This article had originally been written at the solicitation of the *New York Times*, which then failed to publish it. An important document of its era, the article explains the philosophy behind the NMDS, which had four paid staff members and three volunteers, and the scope of its work at the time: distribution to some four hundred stores, contact with 150 radio stations, and a list of 285 records in its catalog. (Ten years later the catalog listed 1,800 records on 340 independent labels.) In her article Bley discussed the repertories and aims of a number of independent labels, including CRI, People's Music Works, Opus One, Survival, Desto Records, Choice Records, Finnadar, Oblivion, Tribe Records, Concept, Chatham Square, and several others carried by the service.

Central to the NMDS's mission was its effort to help the music survive, not to earn money, as Marquand made clear. Such was the case with commercially minded record companies, of course, which aimed to make products that would bring in a profit. Taylor Storer, the office manager of the NMDS from 1978 until 1985, remarked that the service would take anything that was independently produced or that could be loosely described as "new music" and that its staff was not concerned with poor sales. Bley's independent nature and creative thinking provided an ideal voice for this operation and aligned her with other composers who had taken publishing, recording, and distribution matters into their own hands during the twentieth century, from Henry Cowell to Muhal Richard Abrams before her to Michael Byron, Peter Garland, Larry Polansky, and John Zorn after her. At the end of "Friendly Independent Record Makers," she poetically conjured up a prevalent image in subsequent descriptions of American independent music. The music was like weeds, she wrote: diverse, unexpected, resilient, and tenacious.

We were the weeds, the wildflowers, the ones who had managed to survive without care.
Long live the new strains
the unknown
the different
the perseverant
the undersized
the oversized
the strangely bent one with its most striking side face down
these mutations
uncared for
clinging to rocks
or cleverly hidden in gardens
some that can only be seen at night
some with unfeasibly large blooms held up by too slender stems
the exceptional
unusual
weird, strange, unfunctional
one of a kind
springing up everywhere
unchecked
listen!

To this poetry she added a dedication: "To John Cage, who recently mentioned that he suspected there were more than the usual number of new green shoots of music coming up around town like Spring." One might well wonder whether the German composer Walter Zimmermann read Bley's essay before giving the name *Desert Plants* to his landmark collection of interviews with American experimental composers published just two years later.[4]

While getting the NMDS up and running and establishing connections with independent record makers worldwide, Bley also ventured into the world of black-tie classical concert music. During the spring of 1974, Bley's work *3/4* was featured in a concert described as "New and Newer Music" at Lincoln Center's Alice Tully Hall, performed alongside other "crossover" works by Ornette Coleman and Frederic Rzewski. Critical discussions about her music at this juncture aligned her with a new strain of Third Stream composition that included a deemphasis on improvisation and a reconsideration of carefully planned structural form. The work had been commissioned by a New York–based group called the Ensemble, which specifically requested a piece for piano and chamber orchestra. The resulting piano concerto explored one of Bley's most beloved and enduring genres: the waltz. As her first experience working with conservatory-trained musicians, the collaboration was not without friction, and she found that classical musicians conceived the notion of personality in music quite differently than did improvisers. The conductor Dennis Russell Davies premiered *3/4* with Keith Jarrett at the piano. It was later performed by Bley's pianist friend Ursula Oppens with the group Speculum Musicae. Bley herself recorded the work for a Watt release that also included Mantler's composition *13*. (Bley has somewhat contradictorily remarked, on separate occasions, that she thought *3/4* was one of the few "perfect" things she had ever done but also that she did not like the recording she made of it.) The following year, in 1975, Jazz Composers Orchestra activities permanently ceased, and Bley's work started to follow new paths. In 1975 Gary Burton made a quintet recording (with Pat Metheny, Mick Goodrich, Steve Swallow, and Bob Moses) called *Dreams So Real*, an album devoted entirely to Bley's compositions that, because of Metheny's popularity, helped her music reach a wider audience.

Nonetheless, the New Music Distribution Service had been central to her work during the 1970s, and in 1978 Bley described the service in this way:

> We believe in the distribution of independent records, and we operate as a non-profit service; we can't depend on getting government or subsidy money, so we run the office as a small business trying to break even to survive. We distribute over 200 labels—without any exclusive agreements—and when there's too much work for us, we cut it off. We've had to get rid of our most successful records, like Chick Corea's *Return To Forever*, Gil Scott Heron's *Winter In America* and the whole ECM line. Distributing them was just too much for our small operation. I don't think there's anything wrong with graduating from NMDS to the big time. There's a machine that serves commercial music very well, but new music or art music not at all, and a machine must be concocted to serve that. This is not your typical capitalist office. We believe in art and expression. Business is an art form I'm trying to learn.[5]

The New Music Distribution Service itself did, in a sense, graduate to the "big time." The 1986 catalog featured original cover art by the highly successful graffiti artist Keith Haring, and in a section entitled "Forewords," Gregory Tate wrote: "Some folks probably just think of the New Music Distribution Service catalogue as this encyclopedic warehouse stocked with mostly independently recorded jazz and contemporary European American classical music. . . . The more savvy perhaps see it as a networking resource for producers, performers, and composers of experimental music." He closes this introduction in whimsical words reminiscent of Bley's own poetic explications about the service: "Even if you never hear more than a fraction of the music available in this catalogue, take it for what it is on its own merits: a trans-dimensional road map to the alternative music of the spheres. Not to mention, one of the funniest documents late postmodernism has yet produced. If not a source of sonic salvation as yet untapped by any known evangelical order. Get it while it's heretical."[6]

7 | *Big Band Theory*

The Carla Bley Band
and Other Projects

IN 1974 BLEY AND MANTLER moved to the isolated rural community of Willow, New York, in the Hudson River valley region of the Catskills, near the legendary town of Woodstock. Bley bought a house there with the profit she had turned by selling her land in Maine. The couple built a private professional-quality sixteen-track recording studio in their basement. Named for the stream and closest identifiable road in this remote area, their "Grog Kill Studio" has been the location for nearly all Bley's subsequent nonlive recording projects up to this day; the couple also rented time in it to other musicians. One such project deepened Bley's connection to the international community of progressive rock musicians, particularly in Great Britain: during October 1976 John Greaves and Peter Blegvad recorded their progressive rock concept album *Kew. Rhone.* at the Grog Kill Studio (the album was released in 1977 by Virgin Records). Bley sang and played tenor saxophone on the record; Mantler played trumpet and trombone. It has since taken on the status of an underground cult classic.

Soon after settling in Willow, in late 1974, Bley joined the Jack Bruce Band, a quintet that included Bruce Gary, Ronnie Leahy, and the Rolling Stones guitarist Mick Taylor, and began rehearsals for a tour. Bruce, who had been aware of Bley's compositions from a relatively young age, encouraged her participation in the band: "I really thought Carla was very special—still do—a very interesting composer, and I just wanted people to be aware of her. I didn't know what she'd

58 be like in the band. But we had done things on *Escalator* where she had an interesting approach to keyboards, very simple. I didn't see her as a technical player, more of a composer who had a particular approach which appealed to me—very Kurt Weill and European."[1]

The tour began on April 22, 1975, in Barcelona, and between then and June 9, when the tour ended at Cambridge University, the group performed twenty-six concerts in nine European countries. On tour Bley mostly played Mellotron and Hammond organ; she left the group when the tour ended. The experience of touring and performing live for large audiences had a transformative effect on Bley, and she became interested in creating her own band. Bley recalls: "Then I joined a famous rock and roll band. That was fun. I hadn't had much fun in my life. I spent a lot of time in Europe. When the group broke up I found it impossible to go back to being a reclusive composer. I wanted to continue traveling and playing in public. So I started my own band. That caused me to write more than ever, since I now had an immediate outlet and a constant demand for new material."[2]

Part of Bley's change in attitude about performing more frequently might also have been influenced by a change in the musical landscape during the 1970s, by which time many musicians recognized the advantages of writing and copyrighting their own material. Steve Swallow, who along with other musicians affiliated with Boston's Berklee College of Music was involved in compiling *The Real Book* around this time, explained that this shift in the roles of players versus composers eroded standards of quality in jazz composition. For the work of a true composer, not just a player who wrote tunes on the side, this new situation was potentially detrimental: "People like Carla [Bley], in particular, who's essentially a writer who plays, rather than a player who writes, suffered mightily. It almost has sounded the death knell of somebody who would call himself a jazz composer. Nobody has any use for a jazz composer anymore, because everybody saw the clear copyright advantages to writing their own tunes, however feeble they might have been, to record."[3]

Perhaps in response to this situation, around 1977 Bley and Mantler published a Watt catalog in the form of a meticulously designed booklet that included several informative, self-promotional descriptions and a strong assertion of their artistic discipline and self-reliance: "Carla Bley and Michael Mantler are two composers. Unable to accept the economic and musical restrictions imposed by the music business establishment, they decided to control their own lives as much as possible, and now have a record company, a recording studio, publishing companies, and a band, all dedicated to the presentation and realization of their music without compromise."[4]

This document also described the process and purpose of creating the Carla Bley Band, a ten-person big band (brass, reeds, and rhythm section) she had spent several years establishing. She formed this group after the Jack Bruce Band tour, and it became the entity on which she would focus much of her energy for several years. The Carla Bley Band effectively became the instrument for which she composed, the vehicle through which she could let her sonic imagination run free. An unsigned descriptive essay (though probably written by Mantler or by Bley herself) in the Watt catalog booklet stated:

> It was a composer's band, and the total effort would be directed towards interpreting the written music of one person. (Carla claims not to be a player, and expresses herself through her compositions and arrangements. In exchange for control of the form, she lets solo space go to her band—a fair trade.) The musicians had to be excellent readers as well as soloists. They had to add something personal and unique, but not overwhelm the music with their egos. Fortunately, within her large and disparate circle of friends, such musicians were not the exception, and she ended up with some wonderful, if unlikely combinations. Famous, unknown, exciting new talents, comfortable old ones, very tall ones, some quite short, from the purest to the most promiscuous, all the elements sublimely intertwined into one force dedicated to making Carla Bley's music more outrageously beautiful than ever.

This emphasis on formal control, the superb technical skills of her musicians, and individuality within the band characterized her working attitude toward all subsequent large ensemble projects.

The establishment of her own large ensemble following the creation of her recording studio, record label, and distribution service was part of a logical chain of events, one indicating a further step in Bley's ongoing quest for total artistic control in the creation, administration, and dissemination of her music. This freedom allowed Bley to focus on an uninhibited exploration of musical ideas in her compositions. During this period she composed an unusual work titled *Bars* (1977), which is notable in that it has an indeterminate form. The piece comprises eight sections, all but one of which are to be repeated. The first six sections are labeled A through F, and after an initial run through in the written order, the first five lettered parts are meant to be played in any order the performers choose: "Any of the first five sections connects with any other; join them at random. Then join parts of sections, they all connect well." This open form, or "cut-up" technique, was typical of the "mosaic" forms of Henry Cowell and the "mobile form" of Earle Brown but was relatively uncommon in the history of jazz.

Over the next few years the Carla Bley Band toured both Europe (extensively) and the United States (in a brief, seven-gig excursion to second-tier, out-of-the-way places, such as Ypsilanti, Michigan), recorded six albums on Watt between

1977 and 1983 (*European Tour 1977*, *Musique Mecanique*, *Social Studies*, *Live!*, *I Hate to Sing*, and *Heavy Heart*), and contributed a soundtrack of preexisting pieces for a Claude Miller film called *Mortelle Randonee*. Much of the music written for this large ensemble seems to suggest that Bley had undergone a change of heart with regard to both her audience and herself, wanting to stop being, as she put it, "an inward, introspective, unsocial, misanthropic, confused, tormented person."[5] This active pursuit of a new mode of expression went well with the proactive, self-determined approach to managing her career. Gary Burton has commented: "I have always considered Carla a great example of how to market music. Her work is not so directly in the mainstream, so it took ingenuity and original thinking to find ways to get her music in front of people. She has definitely succeeded as an organizer and businesswoman, bringing her music to a much wider audience than would have happened if she had just waited for the audience to find her work."[6]

The Carla Bley Band was indeed successful, in part because it featured entertaining, outrageous, theatrical pieces such as *Spangled Banner Minor*, a twenty-plus-minute medley of national anthems (including "Deutschland über Alles") and "patriotic" pieces by Bley (mostly written during the 1960s) such as *Flags*, *King Korn*, *And Now, the Queen*, and *The New National Anthem* (which had been recorded on *A Genuine Tong Funeral*). The band's personnel, consisting of highly skilled music readers who were also free improvisers, soon became a diverse group of eccentric and original musicians including the AACM-trained trombonist George Lewis, the versatile ONCE festival/Iggy Pop–band pianist "Blue" Gene Tyranny (whom, it is alleged, Bley hired for the European tour just because she liked his unusual name), and the classically trained but virtuosically improvising French horn player John Clark. Bley played primarily organ or synthesizer in her band during this period and frequently hired another musician to play piano parts.

In addition to touring, the band played at the Bottom Line, on Fourth Street near New York University's main campus, and other venues in New York City. The continuity of the Carla Bley Band's personnel gave her a consistently willing and able palette for her compositional explorations, though gender dynamics sometimes led to challenges to her authority. Already a skilled orchestrator, she focused on allowing her creative skills to develop even further. Roswell Rudd, an original member of her first big band, remarked:

> I always felt she was writing a part for me. She had me in mind when she was writing the part. It was a good feeling. I was able to flow in Carla's music. I think she was on the crest as an orchestrator. In other words, she was getting to that Duke Ellington stage where she had the soloist in mind when she was writing stuff, so your part was kind of personalized. Right from the beginning, when the first times I was looking at her charts, I was feeling

that. [She was] right up there with Mingus, and Ellington, and anyone who was orchestrating a soloist. The writing was kind of secondary to what they heard the soloist doing in the orchestral space. The acoustical reality of the performer came first.[7]

He added: "Everybody to a lesser or greater degree in the band was a soloist, was an individual personality, and I think she was able to harness that energy into her soundscape."

After the *European Tour 1977* album, Bley recorded *Musique Mecanique*, which contains some of her most inventive writing and arranging from this period and some of the most extroverted and exuberant performances by her band. The collection—just five pieces played by an enhanced ensemble (she added several players, including Charlie Haden on bass, Eugene Chadbourne on guitar, and Karen Mantler on glockenspiel)—exemplifies her parody-ridden humor, her gift for variation, her theatricality, and her interest in the "acoustical reality" of not only human players but broken machines. The title of the album, and of three of the pieces included on it, refers in part to a display of mechanical musical instruments Bley saw at the Musée Mécanique in San Francisco. She also connects various themes on the record (and in many of her other work) to an idea of brokenness, related to the idea of "imperfection" discussed earlier with regard to her use of amateur musicians and unusual vocalizations in *Escalator over the Hill*. In Bley's music, brokenness becomes a phenomenon worthy of a certain amount of close attention. This phenomenon became central to her style. She recalled: "My style started with a broken toy bought in Chinatown when I was about eight years old. It was a musical toy, but it was broken."[8] These images contribute to a music that is referential, evocative, and sometimes very specific in its imagery; in that sense, it is not unlike romantic program music or any music that aims to tell a story or to set the listener in a particular place—urban gridlock, for example, in the pieces *Fast Lane* and *Tijuana Traffic* (2003), for which the band's brass section effectively turns into a blaring cacophonous pileup of annoyed automobile horns (perhaps a nod to Duke Ellington's depiction of honking car horns in "Take the A Train").

The first piece on the album *Musique Mecanique*, called *440* (referring to a commonly employed frequency for the pitch A, which orchestras use to tune up before playing), is typically humorous, using conventions of classical music itself—and here, in particular, the formalized, repetitive art music rituals so foreign to the candid, cool, dressed-down world of jazz (at least before 1980)—both to call attention to their absurdities and to generate entirely new musical ideas. The band begins by improvising solely on the pitch A, until the thematic part of the piece begins. The second piece on the album is called *Jesus Maria and Other Spanish Strains* and employs another self-referential kind of practice, the use of

Bley's early piece *Jesus Maria* as the ritornello to a suitelike construction. The arrangement includes stylistic replicas of Spanish- and Latin-sounding music, as well as sonic clichés from western movie music (one thinks of cowboys and shootouts almost involuntarily). This arrangement of *Jesus Maria* also includes a variety of bizarre vocalizations and electronic effects including a walkie-talkie.

The second side of the album presents three separate but related pieces collectively titled *Musique Mecanique* (Bley and Swallow later rerecorded the *Musique Mecanique* triptych as an instrumental set on their third duo album, *Are We There Yet?* [1999]). The first of the set includes a collection of music boxes, hurdy-gurdies, glockenspiels, electric pump organs, celestas, and toy pianos. Perhaps a bit rusty from disuse, they take a while to get up to speed; at the end of the ten-minute romp the devices slowly wind down again, until just one remains, clicking and clacking in its unabashed brokenness. The second of the *Musique Mecanique* set, titled *At Midnight*, features Roswell Rudd intoning a dreamlike then increasingly ecstatic circular text written by Bley.[9] (This would be the last record by the band to feature Roswell Rudd; soon thereafter the trombonist Gary Valente would become one of Bley's most cherished soloists, along with the trumpeter Lew Soloff and saxophonists Wolfgang Puschnig and Andy Sheppard.) The piece also makes use of eerie sounds associated with night: a ticking clock, the lonely knelling of a bell, a creepily intoning organ.[10] The third *Musique Mecanique* piece exploits a sonic device that mimics the sound of a record skipping (Bley likely first used this effect shortly before, in the tune *Drinking Music*, on the *European Tour 1977* album): all of a sudden, the players get "stuck" on certain riffs, repeating them precisely—seventeen times in one case and fifteen times in another—until the music lurches forward. The broken-record technique—which is exploited in later recordings, too, most notably in *Tigers in Training*, a lengthy piece making explicit references to the sounds of the circus and included on Bley's 1998 record *Fancy Chamber Music*—further focuses the listener's attention on Bley's fascination with odd sound effects and unexpectedly humorous compositional techniques.

Soon after the Carla Bley Band's inception, the bandleader found herself enjoying the luxury of turning down more engagements than she accepted, even though invitations to perform in the United States were few and far between. Since she earned most of her income through copyright royalties and financed her band in that way (this is no longer the case), she was under no pressure to perform more often than she wished. By 1978, when she recorded *Musique Mecanique*, she was able to live quite comfortably as an established composer, and as in all other aspects of her professional life, she maintained complete artistic and administrative control over her work. She has noted that almost everything she has written has been covered, which has provided her a sizable income.[11] She adds, "I live very comfortably. And I feel proud and sort of like a shining example, mainly because I'm independent. I don't belong to a stable. I'm not a pet of the recording industry. I put out my own records. We book our own band. I have my publishing company. I have my own recording studio. Everything I do is totally controlled by me. [. . .] I've never had to compromise one bit."[12]

This independence gave her an almost unprecedented amount of freedom for a composer insistent on writing in original and not necessarily mainstream idioms. This freedom has allowed Bley to interact with an astounding variety of musical milieus since the mid-1970s, even as she was leading her band. These additional projects included, among other things, fulfilling diverse types of commissions (including one from Germany's WDR television to create a piece accompanying the poetry of Malcolm Lowry; the result—For *Under the Volcano*—with Steve Swallow and Jack Bruce, was performed first in Cologne and later as part of the New Music America Festival); recording John Cage's songs "The Wonderful Widow of Eighteen Springs" and "Forever and Sunsmell" on Brian Eno's Obscure label (1976); participating in a symposium at the Woodstock Creative Music Foundation in 1977 (along with Cage, Frederic Rzewski, and Christian Wolff); collaborating with avant-rock figures such as Jack Bruce, Robert Wyatt, and the former Pink Floyd drummer Nick Mason (for whom she wrote, arranged, conducted, and recorded an entire album, *Fictitious Sports*, at her studio in 1979; it was released under Mason's name two years later); and playing the role of a keyboardist named "Penny Cillin" in an irreverent punk band called Burning Sensations with Peter Apfelbaum and others associated with Karl Berger's Creative Music Studio in Woodstock. The scholar-performer George Lewis, who played in the Carla Bley Band during its first European tour, in 1977 (but did not play on the subsequent record), has suggested that Bley was able to maneuver gracefully among these many different musical styles and performance projects because a certain tolerance for stylistic mobility has traditionally been granted to white artists but not to musicians of color—for example, the African American composers Scott Joplin, Duke Ellington, Muhal Richard Abrams, and Anthony Braxton, whose stylistic border crossings met with incomprehension or worse from a critical establishment that expected them to stay within an aesthetic position it identified as "jazz."[13] Bley's stylistic mobility, her creative restlessness, and her identification with multiple traditions and performance practices have caused her to be described, on occasion, as chameleon-like.

For a time in the later 1970s Bley provoked audiences with what some critics referred to as punk jazz, taking her big band to Lower East Side venues such as

Hurrah's and encouraging listeners to boo her on stage. (She has admitted that her irreverent and repetitious songs on Nick Mason's *Fictitious Sports* album were influenced by the punk rock movement, and the punk band Burning Sensation played many of these songs, including one she called *It's Rotten*, which she jokingly referred to as a "dentist's song.") She also contributed to a number of collaborative recordings organized by other people, including the Conjure recordings of Kip Hanrahan, which set Ishmael Reed's texts to music, and the producer Hal Willner's Kurt Weill and Thelonious Monk collections. Around 1980 Bley's work moved more toward a conversation with traditional big-band jazz. In 1981 she self-published her first collection of printed scores.

A film of a Carla Bley Band performance in Montreal in 1983 documented the working atmosphere of the band at a key creative moment in Bley's long career as a performer.[14] Included in the concert are arrangements of several compositions Bley often recorded during the 1980s, such as the soulful *The Lord Is Listening to Ya, Hallelujah!*; the jerky rhythmic romp *Walking Batterie Woman*; *Ups and Downs*, arranged here as a showpiece duet between the saxophonists Steve Slagle and Joe Lovano; and *The Lone Arranger*, during which Bley and the band, speaking in French, made irreverent comments about horses into their microphones. Bley, her face partially hidden behind her frizzy blond hair, bare-legged and dressed in a bright red shorts-suit, plays keyboards and glockenspiel and occasionally steps in front of the nine-man band to conduct cues. The band itself is playful, polished, and highly virtuosic. Bley's keyboard solos are typically modest, thoughtful, and sparse; a second keyboard player, Ted Saunders, brings a more high-energy, free-jazz style of soloing into the texture. The film, like any live performance by Bley and her band, gives a clear and lasting impression of the wide continuum of the composer's expressive powers and the high level of competence and professionalism of the ensemble that provided the vehicle for bringing those expressive powers to life.

8 | *The Lone Arranger*

History and Hilarity

HUMOR IS NOT USUALLY CONSIDERED to be a prime ingredient in jazz composition or performance, but it is a central component in Bley's music. Through her long career Bley has used satire, parody, irony, slapstick, and pure silliness, often to draw attention to the traditional treatment of certain musical and social conventions. In particular, the Carla Bley Band era (roughly 1977–83) saw her inner comedian run rampant. Bley's composition titles alone have pointed to her affection for the silly (*Blues in Twelve Bars and Blues in Twelve Other Bars, Blunt Object, The Banana Quintet*); strange puns, rhymes, and other wordplay (*Wrong Key Donkey, Strange Arrangement, Song Sung Long, Spangled Banner Minor, Paws without Claws, On the Stage in Cages, High Mass for Low Brass, Liver of Life, Boo to You Too*); musically referential titles (*3/4, 440, Intermission Music, Ad Infinitum, More Brahms, Overtoned, Reactionary Tango, Valse Sinistre, Sing Me Softly of the Blues, Hip Hop, Setting Calvin's Waltz*); and the plain surrealistic or bizarre (*Ida Lupino; Utviklingssang; Sex with Birds; The Girl Who Cried Champagne; Lawns; Fleur Carnivore; And Now, the Queen; Bent Eagle*).

Bley's cover art and liner notes further highlight her fondness for whimsy and slapstick. In one particularly outlandish moment, Bley had the members of her all-male band, clad in red T-shirts, form a human pyramid for the back cover of her *Live!* album. The cover of *4X4* shows her octet sitting in an enormous artillery tank. (That album, recorded in Oslo during a European tour, included a beautiful arrangement of Bley's quasi-Scandinavian ballad *Utviklingssang*.) Irreverence is of course a form of subversion, and Bley uses her peculiar titles, preposterous liner notes, and outrageous cover designs to mock the self-important gravitas of both the compositional world and the recording industry. She admits: "I find it difficult to be reverent about anything obvious (with the exception of certain musical phrases)."[1] She has also said: "Although I've done pretty well at music, I still have never written a joke. I'd like to write a joke someday, but there was more to it than that. What really hit me is that it must mean that music and jokes are totally human. Everything else can be duplicated and programmed, but not music or humor."[2]

Bley's embrace of hilarity by no means indicates music of diminished or superficial quality. On the contrary, her strategic use of humor adds a layer of information that enhances the meaning of the music as a whole. It also frequently intersects with political or politicized themes, especially in her ongoing compositional and orchestration work for Charlie Haden's Liberation Music Orchestra, which has produced four records with overtly political intentions since 1969. Haden has commented that Bley "has a sensitivity to the injustices of the world."[3] The first Liberation Music Orchestra project focused on the civil rights movement, the Vietnam War, and the revolutionary movement in Cuba (*Liberation Music Orchestra* [1969]); the second thematized the ongoing conflicts in Central and Latin America (*Ballad of the Fallen* [1983]); the third concerned the South African struggle to end apartheid (*Dream Keeper* [1990]); and the most recent alluded to the Iraq War and American imperialism (*Not in Our Name* [2005]).

Her typical style utilizes a sophisticated method of musical commentary, playing with both the audience's expectations and with their ability to get the joke. Especially in the music with political references, incongruous juxtapositions often heighten her candidness, as do musical quotations (of, e.g., Beethoven's Fifth Symphony, patriotic songs, Frédéric Chopin, a baseball organ riff, Thelonious Monk, the Beatles, Dizzy Gillespie's popular bebop tune "Salt Peanuts," and Gershwin's "Someone to Watch over Me" at the end of her piece titled *Someone to Watch*). Members of her bands also take liberties with quotation: in the final moments of the *Sex with Birds* section of the suite *Wildlife* (recorded on Bley's 1985 album *Night-glo*), for example, Steve Swallow whimsically inserted a few phrases from Bley's composition *Ida Lupino*.

Humor and reference function in varying ways in both Bley's compositions and her ensembles' live performances, and many of her pieces contain multiple layers of both musical and extramusical meaning. One such work is *Ups and*

Downs, written for her friend Taylor Storer during his battle with cancer. Storer, a legendary concert producer for Columbia University's WKCR and a driving force behind the New Music Distribution Service, died in 1985. The title *Ups and Downs* refers literally to the musical motion of the piece (an aimless, constantly oscillating melody); at the same time, it refers to the drastic and exhausting ups and downs of a terminal cancer patient. In this simple way, Bley simultaneously draws attention to both the superficial corniness of her melody, the mundane aspects of life, and the grim condition of her dying friend.

In a more extroverted mode of expression, one of Bley's funniest moments is a song called *I Hate to Sing*, which was recorded live in San Francisco by the Carla Bley Band and released on a record of the same name in 1983. The campy arrangement has a cabaret sensibility, emphasizing the 4/4 oom-pah feel of a slightly seedy band that sometimes plays as if it were merrily inebriated. The band's drummer, in this case D. Sharpe (his name itself a musical pun), has the humiliating task of singing the song. In Bley's typical way of drawing attention to the immediate musical moment, her lyrics explicitly expose the singer/drummer's intense discomfort with the spotlight, the situation, and his own voice:

I hate to sing
I really hate to sing;
Why do I have to sing?
It's so embarrassing;
I get self-conscious
When the band launches;
Into the intro
Of my big song.

I feel extremely tense
I have no confidence;
What if the audience begins to leave?
I'm not in training
I feel like fainting;
It sure is hot here
I need some water;
My mouth is dry . . .
[The music stops: Sharpe asks for a glass of water and comments humorously on the
    questionable skills of his band.]
[instrumental interlude]

I'll stand up like a man [Sharpe pounds on his chest]
And do the best I can.

[shyly] I'm still not ready
I feel unsteady;
[singing out of tune] I think this melody
Is much too hard for me;
Uh duh duh da da dum dee dum dee dum
I forgot the words.
[Band members chime in loudly, singing "La la la" on the main melody.]

And on it goes. This self-referential jesting—pointing out what is happening onstage at the moment it is taking place—might be considered "postmodern" or perhaps satirical, the situation exaggerated until it becomes clearly absurd. Moreover, by drawing attention to the soloist's anxiety, a condition widespread even among those well accustomed to the stage, Bley depicts the most pedestrian of performers' carefully hidden insecurities. By underscoring something otherwise left tactfully unacknowledged, she gives us permission to take delight in a human quality reinterpreted as something endearing rather than a shameful flaw. (*The Watt Works Family* booklet, published by Watt Works and ECM in 1990, included a "trial transcript" in which Bley defends herself before a judge who interrogates her about her "crime" of releasing the album *I Hate to Sing*.) In a similar vein, Bley's song *Very, Very Simple* contains lyrics that have Steve Swallow, for example, singing about what he is singing while using only one pitch throughout the entire song: "Here's a very simple melody / that Carla wrote especially for me / She said: 'Everyone according to his ability' / And then she gave the simplest one to me. / If I concentrate I know I won't go wrong / And then maybe some day / [spoken] I'll get a better song." The effect is self-effacing, musically erudite, and quite funny.

In a comic style possibly inspired by Victor Borge's reading a sheet of piano music upside-down, Bley's *Piano Lesson* parodies a beginning piano student repeatedly trying to play a major scale.[4] Again and again we hear the scale begin correctly—do, re, mi, fa, so, la—only to run astray with wrong notes near the end—bleep, blat! Why is it so humorous? Why would such a skilled composer deliberately write "wrong" notes? (Bley has said that the piece has a plot: "I play a stern music teacher teaching scales; three players start a mutiny and I end up joining them.")[5] As have other musical comedians before her, Bley plays with our expectations in the simplest way possible, by denying our ear the "proper" resolution, and the aural punch line allows us to laugh at a "mistake." Bley turns the curse of bad piano playing into a delightful quirk to be celebrated. Such musical jokes suggest fond memories from her youth (listening to her father teach piano lessons at home) while simultaneously hinting at Bley's professed lifelong sense of insecurity at the piano.

Some of Bley's other irreverent efforts in writing and arranging stem from her "punk-jazz" phase in the late 1970s, when Bley worked with Nick Mason to produce the eight songs that became *Nick Mason's Fictitious Sports*. Far from being a typical rock band, nearly all the fifteen musicians involved in this album belonged to Bley's inner circle: Mantler, Swallow, Howard Johnson, Terry Adams, Gary Valente, Gary Windo, D. Sharpe, and others. Robert Wyatt of the band Soft Machine sang lead vocals on seven of the eight tracks (Mason had produced Wyatt's solo album *Rock Bottom* in 1974). The last and longest song on the record, called *I'm a Mineralist*, contains a lengthy passage in the repetitive, tonal, metrically shifting choral style featured in Philip Glass's minimalist opera *Einstein on the Beach* (1976). Both the song lyrics and the musical style rely on the listener's ability to associate the word *mineralist* with the word *minimalist*, as the static single phrase of the melody moves as a unit between two adjacent pitches throughout. The text that introduces the Glass parody refers explicitly to other music that might be considered minimalist and to which Bley was devoted: "Erik Satie gets my rocks off, Cage is a dream." This is followed by the rhyming phrase "Philip Glass is Mineralist to the extreme." Then the band abruptly switches to the *Einstein on the Beach* reference: tonal harmony, arpeggiated chords, a metrical shift from 4/4 to 5/4, and an earnest group chant of "aah." This goes on for quite some time, long enough for it to take on an even greater comic significance within the context of the already humorous song. The chorus reappears during the song's, and the album's, dramatic coda.

In her work with the Liberation Music Orchestra, Bley found herself most squarely in the role of "lone arranger." She has arranged and orchestrated nearly all the music for that ensemble since its inception. This includes original music by Haden, Ornette Coleman, Hanns Eisler, Pat Metheny, Bill Frisell, Antonin Dvořák, and Samuel Barber, as well as Spanish Civil War songs, Central and South American folk songs, "Amazing Grace," "We Shall Overcome," the Chilean protest song "El Pueblo Unido Jamás Será Vencido," and "America the Beautiful," into which she embedded the African American song "Lift Every Voice and Sing." In addition to undertaking this massive amount of orchestration, Bley also composed seven individual pieces for the group, including her seventeen-minute *Dream Keeper* suite (titled for the Langston Hughes poem), which utilizes music from Spain, Venezuela, and El Salvador.

Though Bley has not frequently voiced her political views as openly as the group's founder, Charlie Haden, has done, the amount of energy she has donated to this cause for over forty years—arranging nearly thirty pieces, several of which are multisectioned suites, for anywhere from ten to seventeen players, not to mention the entire Oakland Youth Chorus for *Dream Keeper*—speaks to her support of Haden's overt and outspoken leftist agenda and his engagement with themes such as revolution, oppression, imperialism, and patriotism from the Vietnam era to the present. And Haden has said that the Liberation Music Orchestra was formed for the express purpose of creating "an active political (and historical) conscious-ness through music."[6] An original spiritual by Haden included as the last tune on the third Liberation Music Orchestra record is unabashedly dedicated to Martin Luther King, Medgar Evers, and Malcolm X (near the end of this arrangement, Bley gloriously lets loose on a gospel-inflected piano solo that reveals her church-steeped musical roots). Of his appreciation for Bley's musical gift and her dedica-tion to his projects, Haden has written: "She is the only person I have ever trusted or will ever trust to arrange the music for the Liberation Music Orchestra."[7]

Haden, whose involvement with Bley stretches from their initial meeting in 1957 through countless performances and recording projects, including *Escala-tor over the Hill*, is widely considered one of the greatest jazz acoustic bass play-ers who has ever lived, and the unique and instantly recognizable sound of his expressive playing has captivated the many dozens of musicians with whom he has closely collaborated. In turn, his appreciation of Bley's orchestrations has been unwavering. He equates her compositional ear to that of Charles Ives, given her upbringing within a Christian musical tradition that has remained a consistent element of her musical career: "The music she was exposed to, and her ear, and her gift," Haden says, are what make her special. At the same time, Haden admits that the harmonies and chord voicings in her music sometimes sound more Euro-pean than American; he invokes the music of Claude Debussy, Darius Milhaud, Maurice Ravel, and Erik Satie—French impressionists who painted pictures in sound using parallel chords, static harmonies, modal melodies, and evocative sonic storytelling techniques. In this sense, he remarks, "She found a way to bring out so many things, in so many ways: sight, emotion, joy, sadness, color."[8]

Bley is often put in the company of other great arrangers—especially Duke Ellington and Charles Mingus, in the assessment of Nat Hentoff. Her facility in instrumental combinations and harmonic voicings, as well as the wide range of emotional expressivity and stylistic variety at her disposal, draw attention to the fine line between "composing" and "arranging" and to the slippery definition of each discipline in the case of artists who excel at both. For her part, Bley finds creative freedom in her instrumental and combinatorial choices, whether she is arranging her own material or someone else's. She uses instrumentation as a key to stylistic allusion and humorous gestures: exaggerated trombone slides, trumpets whinnying like horses, screaming choruses of reeds, flamenco guitar, funk-infused bass, reggae drum patterns.

Her sonic choices are used to underscore deeply serious historical themes, too. Sometimes she merely juxtaposes disparate sounds within an emotionally charged texture, as in her rendition of the African National Congress's anthem on the third Liberation Music Orchestra record, when an African chorus underlies Dewey Redman's energetic solo. An intriguing instance of her (and Haden's) tactical deployment of "found sound," or prearranged and prerecorded music, can be heard in the twenty-minute suite near the beginning of the first Liberation Music Orchestra album, recorded in 1969. The remarkably diverse thirteen-person ensemble allowed for maximum sonic experimentation, for it included not only the standard brass, reeds, and rhythm sections but also Indian wood and bamboo flutes, French horn, wood blocks, bells, Tanganyikan guitar, and thumb piano. The suite, titled *El Quinto Regimiento—Los Cuatro Generales—Viva la Quince Brigada*, was based on Spanish folk songs that had been fitted with new revolutionary words during the Spanish Civil War in the 1930s. Bley's setting of the suite features waltzes in the style of brass street bands, the vigorous and virtuosic strumming technique of flamenco guitar, rattles, shouting, and extended sections of free jazz—including a playful trombone solo by Roswell Rudd. Haden has described a feature of the work that reveals its historical connection: "We use[d], with only slight changes, the original 1930 orchestra and chorus arrangements of 'Los Cuatro Generales' and 'Viva La Quince Brigada' as they were playing on the sound track of the film *Mourir à Madrid (To Die in Madrid)*. Parts of these same arrangements from that sound track are super-imposed under the improvising on 'Los Cuatro' and 'Viva.'"[9]

The inclusion of original recordings from the 1930s—the first during Rudd's solo and the second during an exalted solo by Gato Barbieri—combined with free improvisation made Haden's first Liberation Music Orchestra album somewhat unique in the jazz world of the late 1960s and explicitly pointed to a direct link between political movements of his time and those of the past. Haden's original composition *Song for Che* on the same album likewise includes a fragment from a preexisting recording, establishing a similarly effective link to the interrelated universal struggles of other times and places. The first Liberation Music Recording also features one of Bley's most vibrant recordings as a soloist, which occurs in their performance of her arrangement of Ornette Coleman's composition *War Orphans*.

One of Bley's most brilliant orchestrations occurs at the end of this same recording. The piece in question, written in response to the events of the 1968

Democratic National Convention in Chicago, is twofold: the first part, a composition by Haden called *Circus '68 '69*, depicts in sound the violence that occurred on that occasion; the second part is Bley's stunningly straightforward arrangement of "We Shall Overcome," with Rudd's trombone carrying the melody. Haden has written:

> The idea for Circus '68 '69 came to me one night while watching the Democratic National Convention on television in the summer of 1968. After the minority plank on Vietnam was defeated in a vote taken on the convention floor, the California and New York delegations spontaneously began to sing We Shall Overcome in protest. Unable to gain control of the floor, the rostrum instructed the convention orchestra to drown out the singing. "You're a Grand Old Flag" and "Happy Days are Here Again" could then be heard trying to stifle We Shall Overcome. To me, this told the story, in music, of what was happening in our country politically. Thus, in Circus we divided the orchestra into two separate bands in an attempt to recreate what happened on the convention floor.[10]

As the "circus" escalates in Bley's arrangement, band members loudly blow whistles, evoking the stampede of the police force. Amid this chaos, the melodic phrases and harmonies from "We Shall Overcome" can be barely detected, a cry for peace suffocating underneath the riot as manifested by the divided orchestra. Fragments and phrases of the tunes Haden names—"You're a Grand Old Flag" and "Happy Days Are Here Again"—burst forth. The result is an amazingly clear sonic snapshot of an unfortunate event preserved in the collective consciousness of several generations of Americans. Despite the aural assault of the "circus," there is nothing remotely pessimistic in Bley's interpretation of the civil rights movement's most enduring song. The first Liberation Music Orchestra album ends on a hopeful if also revolutionary note. For the cover art, the band was photographed under a large red banner, with Haden holding one end of the pole and Bley holding the other.

Bley's political sensibilities remain an important aspect of her work. In an on-line essay entitled "Carla Bley Profiles Herself," the composer makes some of her most explicit statements about world affairs, notably, her opposition to policies implemented by the George W. Bush administration and the Iraq War. She describes herself in this way: "I'm a typical *New York Times* reading, National Public Radio listening, left-leaning liberal. I vote Democrat whether I like the candidate or not." As an engaged citizen of the United States, Bley reflects on national themes through various medley-like pieces that combine anthems and patriotic songs with her own compositions that feature titles evocative of nationalistic sentiments.

Bley's suite *Spangled Banner Minor and Other Patriotic Songs* pitted her early pieces *Flags*, *And Now, the Queen*, *King Korn*, and *The New National Anthem* against a collage of national anthems rewritten in minor keys. She has remarked that she wrote *Spangled Banner Minor* to express "some disappointment or other with the United States government" and that it is "very sad and very political."[11] The piece is rich with references, and simple instrumental choices bring into high relief some strange associations, such as the similarities between the opening of the "Star-Spangled Banner" and Beethoven's "Appassionata" Sonata. In another instance, "Yankee Doodle" is heard in close proximity to the German national anthem, "Deutschland über Alles" (also played in minor). A minor-key "Marseillaise" marches through in all its declamatory, dotted-rhythm glory. "Deutschland über Alles" also serves as a chorale-like carpet underneath a rowdy and very free saxophone solo. Soon thereafter, a minor version of "My Country 'Tis of Thee"—otherwise known as "God Save the Queen"—serves as an introduction to Bley's *And Now, the Queen*. During the final third of the piece, a hymnlike tune favored by many American universities as their school song looms large.[12] Throughout, military-style drumming and the inclusion of an electric organ underscore the Americanness of it all, despite the presence of an array of international anthems. *Spangled Banner Minor* ends with an emphatic blast of John Philip Sousa's "Stars and Stripes Forever," but Bley abruptly concludes the entire piece by quoting the well-known parody version, which is usually accompanied by nonsense lyrics: "Be kind to your fine feathered friends, / for a duck may be somebody's mother. / Be kind to your friends in the swamp / where the weather is very, very damp. / Now, you may think that this is the end, / well it *is*!" Her source material, it seems, is unlimited. The result is a humorous and symbolic symphonic collage of colliding tunes. It is richly referential and peppered with quotation, not unlike Charles Ives's programmatic "Fourth of July" movement from his *New England Holidays Symphony*.

On her 2003 album *Looking for America*, scored for an eighteen-piece band, Bley continued exploring her fascination with collages. The centerpiece of this album is an extended work called *The National Anthem*, a piece she admits had a "patriotic virus" (it includes parts titled "OG Can UC?," "Flags," "Whose Broad Stripes?" "Anthem," and "Keep It Spangled"). The piece begins in a particularly funky style not usually associated with national themes. Typically irreverent yet seriously critical, Bley found that "our poor National Anthem really could use some work." She added, "It wasn't the first time [. . .] I'd been tempted to improve upon one of our patriotic songs." Though the album was released shortly after 9/11, Bley has said that most of the music was written before that event occurred.

On one occasion she insisted that *Looking for America* is not about politics; rather, she said, "it's about music, American music and Latin music."[13] In her on-line essay about the album, she wrote: "This album isn't just about the United States. America encompasses two continents. I'm focusing on the original and transformed music that has come out of this vast region." Further, the recording is treated like a concept album in that it is linked by short sections of recurring music titled "Grand Mother," "Step Mother," "Your Mother," and "God Mother"; mother, perhaps, represents the homeland, America. The album closes with Bley's arrangement of "Old MacDonald Had a Farm."

Finally, for the most recent Liberation Music Orchestra recording, *Not in Our Name* (2005), titled after the national project founded in 2002 to mobilize resistance to the Bush administration's "war on terror," Bley arranged another medley, this one called *America the Beautiful*. This suite includes arrangements of the songs "America the Beautiful" (in minor rather than the original major), "Lift Every Voice and Sing," and a section, introduced by a drum solo, of Ornette Coleman's 1972 "concerto grosso" for jazz band and orchestra, *Skies of America*. As a companion piece to the large-scale, interconnected works *Spangled Banner Minor*, *The National Anthem*, and *United States* (included on *The Very Big Carla Bley Band* recording of 1990), *America the Beautiful* carries further Bley's devotion to the songs that are profoundly symbolic, and often fraught, within the United States and around the globe. The *America the Beautiful* medley ends poignantly and ominously with a trumpet holding a tone. Clocking in at seventy-five minutes of music, these four patriotic suites constitute a significant compositional commitment on Bley's part. These engaging programmatic works offer a special opportunity to reflect on the role America's music has played within Bley's own compositions.

Whether discussing Bley's use of humor, parody, audacity, quotation, preexisting musical material, or political commentary, we might consider the degree to which one can hear her underlying ideological concerns within the egalitarian treatment of her musical sources. Roswell Rudd felt that their generation's greatest cultural concerns—civil rights, the Vietnam War, equality, and collectivity—led to a musical community that was all-encompassing. People were not black or white, women or men, not composers or improvisers or rock stars, but just people coming together to create something greater than themselves. For Bley, who was fortunate to be surrounded by many talented musicians who believed in these ideals, that creation was big enough to encompass both serious messages and lighthearted fun. In her composing and arranging, history and hilarity go hand in hand.

9 | *End of Vienna*

Fancy Chamber Music

IN 1974, WHEN BLEY WROTE 3/4, the piano concerto commissioned by the New York group the Ensemble, she delved into composing for classically trained musicians for the first time. The title of the piece refers to the triple meter typical of a waltz. Scored for chamber orchestra (including two percussionists, melodic and nonmelodic, and an orchestral pianist in addition to the piano soloist), 3/4 starts out as a slow minor waltz, with short two-bar cells that are repeated several times. Combining her affection for the waltz with her fondness of the mechanical, Bley has the drums create sound effects she describes in the score as "windings, creakings," "rattlings, tickings," and "whirrings, grindings." The perpetual-motion plodding of the second piano is strict and repetitive, providing unity to the piece. The other instruments are treated as fleeting soloists, changing the orchestral color as they move in and out of the foreground. The solo piano part is dictated to an extent by key, scale, or chord changes; sometimes the pianist is instructed to provide "light fill" in a particular key; sometimes the music is written out and doubled by the second pianist. Following a conventionally placed cadenza, the final section has the soloist improvising over chord changes before the ensemble winds down, echoing the opening with its windings, rattlings, and tickings. The 3/4 meter is maintained religiously throughout, and the piece is adventurous harmonically but not rhythmically (one reviewer compared its relentless rhythmic drive to that of Maurice Ravel's *Bolero*).[1] Aside from the solo piano part, played at the premiere by Keith Jarrett, all the other parts are intended to be read directly from written-out parts. Perhaps this relatively conservative approach to the scoring of *3/4* reflected Bley's hesitancy to ask classical musicians to improvise and her lack of confidence then in the ability of conservatory-trained players to handle complex material. Up to that point in her career, her primary musical collaborators had been musicians trained in the collaborative and improvisatory styles of jazz or rock.

Though many of Bley's non-big-band compositions are chamber music of some kind, since the mid-1980s she has occasionally worked in a category she calls "Fancy Chamber Music." Compositions in this category—currently about ninety minutes of music scored for flute, clarinet, violin, viola, cello, bass, piano, vibes, and percussion—consist of fully notated pieces for nonimprovising musicians. In 1996 Bley released the record *Fancy Chamber Music*, which includes six works played by an octet. The booklet accompanying the CD of this recording relentlessly spoofs the conventional pretensions of classical music culture—the sort of thing one finds, for example, in program booklets at the Lincoln Center—by including high-end advertisers or corporate sponsors with addresses on Fifth Avenue, phony companies (e.g., "Tournoff" watches and "Hole" investment advice), and a list of administrators (Ilene Mark, who manages Watt Works, is listed as "Chairman of the Development Committee"; Timothy Marquand and Wolfgang Puschnig are listed as "Chamber Music Program Co-Chairs"). Though the "Chamber Music Annual Fund" includes a disclaimer that "costs require that [it] limit [the] listing of donations to those of $1 and above," it goes on to list just two categories of contributors: the Golden Circle (donations of $500,000 or more) and the Silver Circle ($500,000 or less). Listed as Golden Circle donors are, among others, the Alrac Music Endowment Trust (a reference to Bley's self-publishing organ), the Watt Family Foundation Charitable Trust, and Editions for Contemporary Music (i.e., ECM). Despite the silliness of the recording's presentation—a piano-playing Bley in a formal black dress and elbow-length fingerless gloves graces the cover—and its overt mockery of classical music's elitism and self-conscious rituals, Bley's pieces of "Fancy Chamber Music" are serious compositions in their own right.

This body of work included a piece called *Coppertone* (though that work does not appear on the *Fancy Chamber Music* record), commissioned by the Lincoln Center Chamber Music Society in 1986, and several quintet arrangements of compositions from a set of eight solo piano pieces dedicated to Ursula Oppens, Alan Feinberg, and Robert Shannon (1987; reorchestrated 1997). Oppens premiered the set in 1988. Named *Romantic Notions*, these pieces strip the music down to its essentials, revealing a great sensitivity to subtle gestures and favorite sonorities. The pieces are "notions" in the sense of romantic ideas, not necessarily true, or in the sense of small useful items, as Bley explained on Marian McPartland's radio program. In their brevity, they are reminiscent of Bley's early "miniatures"; the individual pieces should each take about one minute to play. All eight pieces are notated without key signatures.

Romantic Notion no. 1, just twenty-two bars long, is slow, quiet, sparse, and enigmatically elliptical (see fig. 8). Its frequent meter changes and the ever-varying

Figure 8. *Romantic Notion no. 1*. Copyright 1987, Alrac Music. Used by permission of Carla Bley.

placement of the repeated two-eighth-note motive add an element of unpredict-ability. The relative immobility of the left hand and the proliferation of rests make the piece seem like a private moment of fleeting thoughts. (An immobile left hand has often shown up in her scores since the early 1960s.) The work resembles Bley's early piece *Floater* to some extent, and it is also quite similar in style to the American composer Morton Feldman's last solo piano work, *Palais de Mari* (1986), written just one year before Bley's set. Like *Palais de Mari, Romantic Notion no. 1* has a particular abstractness, evoking a sense of irregularity, gentle-ness, and space.

The second work in the set is quicker and establishes a syncopated pattern that carries through most of the piece. It is gradually embellished with melodic figures and chords and then followed by a freer cadenza-like section marked *rubato*. Not unlike some of Bley's early works (in particular, *Walking Woman* and *And Now, the Queen*), *Romantic Notion no. 3* provides a microscopic, bare bones glimpse into her musical values. Bley's rendition of this piece on the first Bley-Swallow *Duets* album (1988) is the best indication of the way she conceptualizes its understated power in performance, playing it in a style highly evocative of Thelonious Monk. This piece, too, has a thin texture, and the regularity of the pulse is disturbed by a further manifestation of what might be called her "broken toy aesthetic," which is worked out here on several levels: the pull between four and five and the resulting disruption of a sense of steady time. This irregular plodding is interrupted three times by wide ascending lines and twice by slow descending glissandi. (The glis-sandi provide a further nod to Monk and his fondness for descending whole-tone runs.)[2] Like some of her early works, these pieces, with musical elements distilled into a limited number of movements, are striking examples of Bley's harmonic vocabulary, her feel for time, and her sense of humor.

The thematic material of *Romantic Notion no. 4* is closely related to the coda of number 2 with its wandering, unaccompanied melodic lines and long rests. These isolated gestures make the music seem fragmentary, without a sense of pulsed continuity. The time is flexible, giving the piece an improvisatory feel. Number 5 is very fast and unified by a syncopated ostinato groove. Over this pattern the right hand seems to take a solo, leaving much space. Of the eight parts to *Romantic Notions*, this piece most closely resembles traditional jazz piano playing. The sixth element is a short waltz like the stumbling march-step moment in *Intermission Music*, and number 7 is pattern based, though static, with a slow sequential melody in the right hand and a series of tied chords in the left that initially reiterate the ostinato pattern in *Romantic Notions no. 5*.

The final piece of the set, number 8, is the shortest, lasting just seventeen bars (see fig. 9). It sounds a great deal like one of Bley's early "songs without words" and is the most traditionally tuneful of the set. Here again, however, time is stretched in unpredictable ways through constant meter changes and a harmonically static left-hand part. The tune stands out in the treble register, but the lower-range harmonies are key to the profile of her sound. The melody is entirely in a major key and sounds like a familiar yet unidentifiable folk song, but the left-hand chords mischievously create a murky dissonance against the lyrically sentimental tune. There is only one instance of an unencumbered tonic triad, which occurs fleetingly, for one brief beat, five bars before the end. This piece, and thus the whole collection, ends with the same simplicity that characterizes the gesture featured in

8

Figure 9. *Romantic Notion no. 8.* Copyright 1987, Alrac Music. Used by permission of Carla Bley.

the first piece of the set. All in all, Bley's *Romantic Notions* reveals the same things that her early pieces did almost thirty years before: two sides of a coin, different places on a spectrum between pulsed patterns and harmonic color, tunefulness and abstraction.

Another piece of "Fancy Chamber Music" from this period is an arresting octet, scored for classical instruments plus vibraphone, called *End of Vienna* (1995; commissioned by the Norddeutscher Rundfunk). The piano plays perpetually arpeggiated eighth notes throughout, and the bass plays sustained pitches. The other instruments enter with melodies that expand and soar and gradually overlap in carefully crafted counterpoint. *End of Vienna* shares some elements in common with *3/4*, though in general it is a more successful ensemble piece, with the parts better integrated and a tighter sense of formal direction. *End of Vienna* is not a waltz, and Bley has written this explanation of its title: "Because it isn't a waltz . . . it marked the end of a disturbing propensity to write pieces in three-quarter time."[3] Certainly its title, its classical instrumentation, and to some degree its smooth and homogeneous sound make reference to Bley's relationship to classical music, particularly the waltz, Brahms, and Vienna itself as that tradition's capital. (Recall that Bley's second husband, Michael Mantler, was a native of Vienna, where she spent time with his family.)

The waltz has occupied a special place in Bley's sonic imagination from the beginning of her compositional career; even one of her youthful variations on "Onward Christian Soldiers" was a waltz. Several of her early pieces were cast in the form of waltzes, as was *Intermission Music* (written for *A Genuine Tong Funeral*), and the titular choral number from *Escalator over the Hill*. Her later *Valse Sinistre* (1980) plays with this dance pattern as well. As a "program note" to her piece *Wolfgang Tango*, included on *Fancy Chamber Music*, she wrote: "Europeans living in Argentina often miss the old country. Even while playing a tango a few strains of a waltz might creep into the music if they're not careful." A recent commission, *Over There* (2008), for solo marimba, was also set as a waltz but, as I will discuss later, presents a similar struggle between musical styles. Though Bley explores the qualities of other dances, most notably the tango, she sees the waltz as a poignant symbol of European music, specifically, the Germanic tradition dominated by the cultural center of Vienna.

As she does with all the musical styles she embraces within her compositions and arrangements, Bley engages the European classical tradition fully. Yet she complicates her musical relationship to that tradition through humor, allusion, and recontextualization. She has studied the European classical canon with great discipline (listening to all of Shostakovich over the course of a winter, for example), spends extensive time with specific pieces from the European repertory (such as Brahms's *Fity-one Exercises*, which she practices daily with a metronome), and regularly discovers new passions (recently, Stravinsky's *Symphony of Psalms*). One of her big-band medleys on the recording *The Carla Bley Big Band Goes to Church* (1996) includes an arrangement of the early twentieth-century composer Carl Ruggles's *Exaltation*, and several of the pieces on the fourth Liberation Music Orchestra recording, *Not In Our Name*, are Bley's rearrangements of orchestral evergreens such as Samuel Barber's *Adagio for Strings* and the famous Largo ("Goin' Home") theme from Antonín Dvořák's Ninth ("From the New World") Symphony. Even the titles *Wolfgang Tango, Valse Sinistre, More Brahms*, and *End of Vienna* draw attention to a kind of "otherness," an exoticist treatment of a body of music that she sometimes appears to hold at arm's length yet embraces passionately given the right opportunity. A fine line lies between earnestness and poking fun; speaking of *Wolfgang Tango*, she has said, "[It is] the very essence of what I want Fancy Chamber Music to be—dignified classical music written for earnest, well behaved, conservatively dressed musicians."

Though not technically a piece of "Fancy Chamber Music," a recent through-composed piece for solo marimba titled *Over There* shows how Bley straddles the American jazz tradition and the European classical tradition, as well as her ongoing exploration, since approximately 1966, of inspirations from popular music. Bley includes the following program note to the published score of *Over There* (2008):

> *Over There* could be imagined as a tug between classical waltz feel and jazz waltz feel. The player starts off in a standard Viennese waltz fashion, but before long, a few syncopations are creeping into the left hand and a swing time–feel gradually takes over. Even "rhythm and blues" phrases pop up, although the early form and chord changes remain unchanged. One R&B inspiration was the Holland/Dozier/Holland song recorded by the Supremes, "Where Did Our Love Go?" That song is an early favorite of mine, and there are quotes from it sprinkled here and there, and references to the way the words "Baby Baby" and the background was sung. The title *Over There* is an accidental quote of a World War II [sic] patriotic song. An entertaining discovery was that the title happens to answer the question of the earlier mentioned Supremes song.[4]

She also included a note to the performer instructing that "the difference between the classical and jazz feels should be subtle." Revealing her own ingrained allegiance, however, she also makes clear that "the last four bars should be played with a strong and rhythmic jazz feel, having, so to speak, the final word."[5]

This "final word" does not help to classify, categorize, or define Bley's musical style; no single piece of her compositions, recordings, or collaborative projects possibly could. But it might help shed light on the place where her ears have come to rest most comfortably. After all, she has spent the last several decades diligently practicing her instrument for several hours a day, deliberately learning how to improvise like a "jazz pianist." This discipline is a refrain running throughout her long career: like the locked groove at the end of *Escalator over the Hill*, it continues indefinitely. Whether writing big-band charts, patriotic medleys, or "Fancy Chamber Music," Bley regards her work with earnestness and integrity.

| # *Dreams So Real*

"Jazz Is Really Where
My Heart Now Lies"

THE TWELFTH ANNIVERSARY OF THE New Music Distribu-
tion Service was celebrated with a benefit concert series of four separate shows
on August 26, 1984. The series was sponsored by Joseph Papp's New Jazz at the
Public Theater. Reflecting the makeup of their catalog itself, the benefit's cast
of eclectic downtown characters included not only Bley but also Robert Ashley,
John Cage, Fred Frith, Arto Lindsay, Butch Morris, Henry Threadgill, John Zorn,
Gamelan Son of Lion, and several other groups and individuals. Perhaps signaling the previously mentioned "tectonic change" in marketing concerns endemic
to the music industry following the appearance of music videos and CDs during the early 1980s, that year the catalog announced: "For the first time ever,
we are presenting our records stylistically, within the groupings of New Music,
New Jazz, and Experimental Music." The catalog also included a statement by
the political writer and jazz critic Nat Hentoff, who emphasized the NMDS's
historical connection to Charles Mingus's independent record label Debut and
to Harry Partch's Gate 5 Records. Though Bley was no longer involved with the
administration of the service, her legacy—the ongoing results of her efforts with
Mantler—had helped build a permanent bridge between the world of Partch and
the world of Mingus, so to speak. For the survival and visibility of independent
American music through intrastylistic cohabitation, the legacy of the New Music

Distribution Service is of paramount significance.[1] Hentoff ended his essay with a personal and ideological note that aimed to underscore that particular cultural contribution: "NMDS is an exceptionally valuable network for people who need music to make sense of the world and themselves. And that's an understatement. When I was a kid I used to buy Harry Partch records by mail direct from Harry Partch. It was exciting, getting the music from the musician. I cherished those records—both for what was in them, and the freedom they represented. And that's what NMDS is distributing. Freedom. You see, it is possible." A few years later, in 1988, and shortly before its close in 1991, the NMDS catalog reached a massive 150 pages.

During the mid-1980s Bley turned her attention to smaller ensembles that played in a mellower, more straightforward and jazzier style. For one, she stripped her band down to a sextet, and with the first album by this group (*Sextet* [1987]), she seemed to turn away, at least temporarily, from the evocative sound effects and theatrical antics of recent albums such as *Musique Mecanique* and *I Hate to Sing!* She also began focusing her attention more deliberately on the rhythm section, as represented by the groups' instrumentation (organ, guitar, piano, bass, drums, and percussion). Most significantly, she began playing duos with Steve Swallow, as she had back in the early 1960s at Phase 2 and other West Village coffeehouses. With her new emphasis on smaller groups, she became more conscientious about sharpening her skills as a pianist. Encouraged by Swallow, with whom she practiced extensively, she systematically learned how to play jazz piano over harmonic changes. During a period of many years Bley and Swallow tirelessly worked their way through *The Real Book* and through their own past and present work, exploring a dynamic mode of musical communication between them. Indeed, Swallow's role in Bley's musical career should not be underestimated: from 1959 to the present day, he has been a tireless advocate devoted to promoting and playing her music (see fig. 10.) In 1987, shortly after they embarked on their duo project, Swallow released a record titled simply *Carla* [1987], on which Bley played organ; this marked the second release on the new label XtraWatt, established for the purpose of releasing primarily records by Swallow and Karen Mantler.

These explorations led to three duo records that included music by both Bley and Swallow, *Duets* (1988), *Go Together* (1992), and *Are We There Yet?* (2000). Around the time they released the first of these, Bley composed the solo piano suite *Romantic Notions*, and they included on *Duets* a version of *Romantic Notion no. 3* where the brief solo piano piece is used as a springboard for improvisation. A deeper investigation into the nature of Bley's own pianism seems to have been central to her work during this period and ever since—though during a period

Figure 10. Steve Swallow and Carla Bley at the Essen (Germany) Philharmonie, September 2009. Photographed by Sven Thielmann. Used by permission of Sven Thielmann.

in the 1980s Bley played primarily organ and synthesizer, and she avoided the piano altogether on *Heavy Heart*, *Night-glo*, and other such albums. At the same time, Bley explored her improvisation skills; in her own opinion, a general lack of improvisatory spontaneity had hindered her ability to solo successfully for much of her career. The duets with Swallow had created a deliberately forced exposure (especially in tender, lyrical ballads, such as *Utviklingssang*, which they also recorded on *Duets*), one Bley initially seemed ready to embrace. She now had no band to hide her, no theatrics to distract, no poetry to imply multiple readings, and no recording techniques to separate player from player or players from listener. In the process of developing herself as one-half of the duets, she made the move, as she put it, from "composer's piano" to "performer's piano."[2] In some of these duo recordings, Bley allows her background in church music to shine through; her arrangement of "Soon I Will Be Done with the Troubles of the World," for example, a traditional gospel song frequently sung by church choirs, provides plenty of plagal cadences, a typical resolution at the end of Christian church music phrases, on which Bley can indulgently linger. In its understated charm, this recording complements Bley's soulful, spiritual-like piece *The Lord Is Listenin' to Ya, Hallelujah!* included on the earlier trio album *Songs with Legs*. Bley's pianistic qualities finally emerged as a mature element of her compositional makeup. Analyzing Bley as a musician, we might determine that "upon close scrutiny, it turns out that many of [her] mannerisms served consistent sonic ends," as the scholar Benjamin Givan has written of Thelonious Monk's peculiar yet brilliant pianism, which obviously exerted a large influence on Bley's approach to her instrument.[3] Swallow has called her particular pianism "Basie meets Monk."

Restlessly reinventing herself yet again, Bley established the Very Big Carla Bley Band, which made its first record, recorded live and titled *Fleur Carnivore*, in 1989. A fifteen-piece ensemble, it played somewhat more traditional, sectional big-band charts than the original Carla Bley Band did. She continued, however, to master the large forms: four of the five pieces on this record last ten minutes or longer. (The record was titled for a piece with the same name, commissioned by Norddeutscher Rundfunk in Hamburg on the occasion of the tenth anniversary of the death of Duke Ellington.) She took this group on a European tour while employed as a visiting professor at the College of William and Mary, in Williamsburg, Virginia—the first academic post Bley had ever held. She recorded another performance of the Very Big Carla Bley Band—now with eighteen members—in Ludwigsburg, Germany, in late 1990. The resulting record opened with the flamboyant fifteen-minute composition called *United States*. Though it quotes the melody to the "Star-Spangled Banner" near its end, the work is highly original and features extroverted solos by her expert musicians. During a contrasting slower and lyrical section, she drastically reduced the texture to a transparent chamber ensemble, featuring herself on piano and Swallow on bass while oboe and flute play lyrical melodies. The effect is much like hearing a piece of "Fancy Chamber Music" interrupt a raucous big-band extravaganza.

The following year, after a remarkably productive musical partnership of over twenty-five years, Bley and Mantler separated. That same year, 1991, the NMDS buckled under the weight of a $160,000 deficit and "ended in ruin," as Bley put it, signaling perhaps the end of a golden era for independent music recording and distribution.[4] Less than ten years later, almost 80 percent of the international recording business would be dominated by five companies—Universal, Sony, EMI, Warner/Time Warner, and BMG-Bertelsmann.[5] Bley continued to record either live on tour or at home in her Grog Kill Studio and to produce her records on the Watt label. The Munich-based ECM continued to distribute Watt products.

During the summer of 1991 Bley and Swallow toured Europe as a duo. They have been performing and recording together ever since, in his bands and in any number of small and large groups she leads and for which she composes with a continuing passion and drive. These groups include the octet called 4X4, consisting of her "favorite" horn soloists and her "first choice" rhythm section, and the Lost Chords, a recent quartet she formed with Swallow, Andy Sheppard, and Billy Drummond. One of the most variegated pieces for this group, a thirty-four-minute-long suite called *The Banana Quintet*, also includes the trumpeter Paolo Fresu. The fourth section of the work is centered on an overt quotation of the unforgettable bass line and broken chords that permeate the Beatles' song "I Want You (She's so Heavy)," recorded for their *Abbey Road* album, signaling Bley's ongoing reverence for that band's songwriting skills. Indeed, the suite format continues to provide a vehicle for Bley's experimentation in varied instrumentation and formal designs. Commissioned by the 1992 Glasgow Jazz Festival and originally intended as a string quartet, the twenty-minute suite for big band and solo violin titled *Birds of Paradise*, included on her 1993 album *Big Band Theory*, features the classical violinist Alexander Balanescu, who founded the eponymous Balanescu Quartet.[6] With her growing recognition as a major figure in American music and the increasing diversity of her work, Bley's music is more and more in demand and attracting greater interest worldwide.

In 1996 Bley gathered seventeen players and released a new live album entitled *The Carla Bley Big Band Goes to Church*. The title explicitly addressed her lifelong connection to Christian hymnody, gospel music, and spirituals; the list of the six tracks on the recording is whimsically labeled a "hymnal." Following in the tradition of her settings of the gospel song "Soon I Will Be Done with the Troubles of the World" and her own piece *The Lord Is Listenin' to Ya, Hallelujah!* (which the Carla Bley Band also recorded on its *Live!* album in 1981), several of the compositions on this album exhibit a religious intertextuality. For example, *Setting Calvin's Waltz*, a twenty-five-minute suite commissioned by the Berlin Jazz Festival, employs preexisting hymn tunes; stylistic allusions to religious music occur throughout; one track is itself an arrangement of Carl Ruggles's *Exaltation*; and several works include referential quotations, such as one of the famous "Halleluja" motive from Handel's *Messiah*. Karen Mantler's organ and harmonica playing adds symbolic church color. Several of Bley's most frequently recorded compositions carry quasi-religious titles—for example, *Healing Power*, *A New Hymn*, and the number that ends the *Goes to Church* album, which carries the spiritual-rhetorical question *Who Will Rescue You?* Through recordings such as these, as well as her devotion to the church-inflected organ in many of her arrangements, Bley acknowledges the influence of her father, Emil Borg, who established the foundation for her steady comfort with spiritual and sacred music. (In 1983 Bley had released a private, limited-edition recording called *My Father's Record*, which featured her father playing classical and "sacred" tunes on the piano, including "What a Friend We Have in Jesus," "The Ninety and Nine," "Let the Lower Light Be Burning," and "Crown Him with Many Crowns." Bley's father passed away in 1990.)

Taken as a whole, whatever type of ensemble or music with which Bley is involved, her compositions constitute a body of work in dialogue with both tradition and experiment. Swallow has described her musical eclecticism in this way:

> Despite Carla's insistence that she's just trying to write like [big-band leader] Ernie Wilkins, she ruthlessly rejects cliché in everything she does. [. . .] Over the years she has evolved a personal melodic vocabulary based on unexpected, but entirely logical, intervallic relationships. She has also synthesized a harmonic vocabulary from a variety of sources. She has an extraordinary ear; she was the first person I'm aware of to develop an understanding of Thelonious Monk's voicings, for example. She has perfect pitch, and can sing the notes in the voicings of incredibly dense harmonies. I've heard her do this to music by Charles Wuorinen, perhaps her favorite composer.[7]

The musical techniques of Bley's diverse compositional output are varied, their moods can be edgy or serene, and their powers of expression are vast. They are abstract and narrative, original and full of borrowings. Because of the variety of musical styles cohabitating within her pieces, the label "jazz musician," which music critics to an extent rightly but far too narrowly apply to Carla Bley, fails to adequately address the full range of her compositional prowess; rather, it merely points to the instrumental forces (reeds, brass, rhythm section, etc.) for which she frequently prefers to write. Typical, perhaps, of American composers who became active during the mid-twentieth century, her musical heroes might come from anywhere. And these heroes—Count Basie, Duke Ellington, Thelonious Monk, Teo Macero, Ernie Wilkins, Kurt Weill, Charles Wuorinen, Anton von Webern, Johannes Brahms, Marvin Gaye, Erik Satie, Igor Stravinsky, the Beatles, the Supremes, the anonymous composers of Christmas carols, Béla Bartók (to whose string quartets Karen Mantler recalls listening extensively as a child), to name just a few—creep into her textures with subtle regularity, though random eclecticism is not her goal. Furthermore, Bley has recently acknowledged a significant change in her own stylistic allegiances. Swallow summarizes it this way: "Carla is a relentless autodidact. As she has come to terms with an endless succession of sources, her vocabulary has broadened. But as she has also moved toward a stronger sense of her own musical identity, her focus has narrowed. This paradoxical process has resulted in increasingly better music."[8]

Bley's voracious appetite for music of all kinds has led her to refer to herself as a sponge, though less so in her later years:

> For the sake of curiosity I have listened to everything Charles Wuorinen ever wrote, but I haven't used a single idea or even begun to know how to do the things he does. I've listened to everything that Shostakovich ever wrote, so maybe that would stand a better chance of sneaking in, but it hasn't. Just last year I listened to all Beethoven's piano music, but I haven't used a single note. I think more often I tend to use things like "Jeepers Creepers," which I tend to use a lot; quotes from a pop song or a religious song I heard before I was ten. I was more of a sponge than I am now, and that music has a better chance of coming out in mine.[9]

Perhaps most tellingly, however, this "stronger sense of her own musical identity" in relation to her "endless succession of sources" has led Bley closer to a clear sense of herself as a particular kind of composer. Indeed, she admits that she is now inspired more by Count Basie than by the Beatles, Webern, or Weill and that she has moved far away from, in her words, the "mavericky" aesthetic of *Escalator over the Hill*. "I hate to say more sophisticated," she mused, adding: "Jazz is really where my heart now lies . . . I just want to be a great jazz composer."[10] Though her attitude toward compositional freedom and independence remains more aligned with the avant-garde than with Wynton Marsalis's preservationist agenda in the institutionalized world of Jazz at Lincoln Center, Bley now deliberately connects her music to the great tradition of big-band and swing orchestra composition.

Seventy-four years old at the time of this writing, Bley is more active than ever, and she composes for several hours a day whenever she is at home in Willow, where she lives with Steve Swallow. To date she has almost three hundred works registered with BMI and has participated in well over forty recording projects, twenty-seven of which (to date) are releases in her own name, placing her among the most accomplished composers, band leaders, and recording artists working in America today. This brief life-and-works study has not covered in detail every tour, recording, or award of Bley's long career. It has left out, for example, a series of commissioned works for which she was erroneously never paid (including one work for the Avignon festival in France called *Holy Roller Coaster*), recent covers of her work by internationally known artists (such as the Fredi Luescher, Cécile Olshausen, and Nathanael Su recording called *Dear C.: The Music of Carla Bley* [Altrisuoni AS 134]), and many recent endeavors in her still very active professional life: new ensemble works; frequent touring; the release of the thirty-fifth Watt recording, called *Carla's Christmas Carols*—a beautiful set of arrangements, the second to last of which, "O Holy Night," Bley gradually transforms into a gospel number—and so on. In late 2009 Bley was awarded the German Jazz Trophy for her life's work. The prize committee described her work as eclectic and atypical: "In her compositions and arrangements, she connects elements of jazz, rock, and European modernism in sometimes grotesque and sometimes ironic ways. Both cryptic and poetic texts play an important role in her work. Settled somewhere between the free jazz of the 1970s and simple rock songs, here in Germany her music has helped establish a multigenerational audience."[11] Bley has been consistently celebrated in Europe as an unconventional and original composer capable of reaching an audience beyond conservative jazz aficionados, and she continues to perform there extensively—something that cannot be said with respect to her home country.[12]

Two fairly recent events deserve notice because of their poignantly retrospective nature. First, the 1997 summer performances of *Escalator over the Hill* marked the first occasion that this monumental work had been performed live in the nearly thirty years since its inception. A twenty-four-piece band was joined by four vocalists and included Paul Haines himself on stage. Premiered for four nights in Cologne, it then traveled to Munich and to other festivals in Austria, Italy, and France, where it was videotaped for French television. Though many musicians, critics, and historians consider the work to be one of the most original and representative compositions of the late twentieth century (especially as a Zeitgeist phenomenon, a document of a time during which all styles of music seemed to be intermingling in unprecedented ways), *Escalator over the Hill* has still never been performed live in the United States.

Finally, on the occasion of the 2005 Monterey Jazz Festival, Bley was honored with a commission, for which she composed a suitelike work for her sixteen-piece band. Bley named the twenty-five-minute piece, *Appearing Nightly at the Black Orchid*, for the nightclub in Monterey where she used to play as a teenager shortly before she roamed east to New York. *Appearing Nightly* aimed to evoke images of the smoky jazz clubs of the 1950s where she first encountered the world that would become her life. The dreams of nineteen-year-old Lovella May Borg, listening studiously to the great composers night after night at Birdland, had finally become—as in the title of one of her early pieces—"dreams so real" for the indefatigable Carla Bley.

NOTES

Epigraph

Rafi Zabor, *The Bear Comes Home* (Norton, 1998), 258.

Introduction

1. Charlie Haden, interview with the author, November 30, 2009.

2. Bley's daughter, Karen Mantler, when asked what she thought was most important for readers to take away from this book, remarked: "That she's a *composer*. There should be no confusion about that" (Mantler, interview with the author, September 3, 2009).

3. Since its inception in 1952, *Down Beat* magazine's "Hall of Fame" has included only six women, all of whom were African American, and five of whom were singers; Mary Lou Williams alone represented the pianist-composer-arranger contribution of women in the field. The women included are Billie Holiday (1961), Bessie Smith (1967), Ella Fitzgerald (1979), Sarah Vaughan (1985), Mary Lou Williams (1990), and Betty Carter (1999). Bley has stated that she was not influenced by Mary Lou Williams; see Bley, interview with Frank J. Oteri, "On Her Own: Carla Bley," *New Music Box*, web magazine for the American Music Center, July 1, 2003, http://www.newmusicbox.org/page.nmbx?id=51fp01.

4. Bley qtd. in Howard Mandel, "Carla Bley: Independent Ringleader," *Down Beat*, June 1, 1978, 19.

CHAPTER 1. *Walking Woman*

Epigraph. Bley, autobiographical introduction to *The Music of Carla Bley, Composed and Arranged for Piano* (Willow, N.Y.: Alrac Music, 1981). All subsequent quotations from Bley in this chapter are from this essay unless otherwise noted.

1. Many published and on-line sources incorrectly state Bley's birth year as 1938.

2. Henry Louis Gates Jr. has established "signifying" as foundational for African American cultural aesthetics, and the concept is widely acknowledged as a key element in the practice of jazz; see Gates, *The Signifying Monkey: A Theory of African-American Literary Criticism* (New York: Oxford University Press, 1988).

3. Bley, autobiographical introduction.

4. Ibid. In an interview I conducted with Carla Bley on August 22, 2009, she sang the beginning of one of her early cowboy songs, which had these lyrics: "A cowboy I'd like to be . . . not a sailor who sails on the sea!"

5. Bley, interview with Ben Sidran, in Sidran, *Talking Jazz: An Illustrated Oral History* (San Francisco: Pomegranate Artbooks, 1992), 177.

6. Bley qtd. in Howard Mandel, "Carla Bley: Independent Ringleader," *Down Beat*, June 1, 1978, 18.

7. The English-born Marian McPartland (b. 1922) has been one of the best-known female jazz pianists since the mid-1950s and has hosted the "Marian McPartland's Piano Jazz" show on National Public Radio since 1978.

8. Bley, interview with Sidran, 177.

9. Ibid.

10. Wilfred Dolfsma, *Institutional Economics and the Formation of Preferences: The Advent of Pop Music* (Cheltenham, U.K.: Edward Elgar, 2004), 2.

11. An ad for this concert is reproduced in Paul Bley's autobiography, *Stopping Time: Paul Bley and the Transformation of Jazz* (Montreal: Véhicule, 1999), 53. This seems to be the only time she used the name Karen for a performance, a name she later gave her only daughter.

12. Her birth certificate and the affidavit are reproduced in Charles W. Turner, "I Hate to Sing: The Life and Music of Carla Bley in Her Own Words," M.A. thesis, Rutgers University, 2004.

13. It is not clear when Bley registered this work with the Library of Congress, but she renewed its registration on July 6, 1987. *Solemn Meditation* was the first recording on which Charlie Haden played. Since then he has remained one of this country's most prolific recording artists.

14. Bley qtd. in Sy Johnson, "And Now, the Emerging Wacko Countess . . . Carla Bley!!!" *Jazz Magazine*, Spring 1978, 39.

15. Charlie Haden, telephone interview with the author, November 30, 2009.

16. See Emmett George Price III, "Free Jazz and the Black Arts Movement, 1958–1967," Ph.D. diss., University of Pittsburgh, 2000, 200.

17. Roswell Rudd, interview with the author, November 4, 2009.

18. Cecil Taylor's studio album *Love for Sale* was also released in 1959 but was not considered as radically innovative or influential as were the records mentioned previously—or as would be Taylor's own later recordings, such as *Unit Structures* (1966).

19. Steve Swallow qtd. in Martin Williams, *Jazz Changes* (New York: Oxford University Press, 1992), 113.

20. See Ran Blake, "Jazz," *Morningsider*, September 14, 1961.

21. Liner notes by Chris Albertson, George Russell Sextet, *Stratusphunk*, sound recording, Riverside 9341 (1960).

22. Bley, autobiographical introduction.

CHAPTER 2. *Sing Me Softly of the Blues*

Epigraph. Bley, autobiographical introduction to *The Music of Carla Bley, Composed and Arranged for Piano* (Willow, N.Y.: Alrac Music, 1981).

1. Bley, interview with Frank J. Oteri, "On Her Own: Carla Bley," *New Music Box*, web magazine for the American Music Center, July 1, 2003, http://www.newmusicbox.org/page .nmbx?id=51fp01.

2. Steve Swallow, written correspondence with the author, July 6, 2009.

3. Her omission of bar lines in some of these early pieces might reflect a further influence of Erik Satie, who was one of the first composers to publish piano pieces lacking meter and measure lines.

4. See Igor Stravinsky, *Poetics of Music*, Charles Eliot Norton Lectures (Cambridge, Mass.: Harvard University Press, 1947), chapter 4.

5. Mendelssohn published eight volumes of *Lieder ohne Wörte* (Songs without words) between 1829 and 1845.

6. Charlie Haden, interview with the author, November 30, 2009.

CHAPTER 3. *Social Studies*

1. Marquand qtd. in John Gruen, "What Would the Late George Apley Have Made of It?" *New York Times*, December 26, 1971.

2. For a detailed description and critical analysis of the Jazz Composers Guild activities and interactions, see Benjamin Piekut, "The Jazz Composers Guild and Black Experimentalism," chapter 2 of "Testing, Testing . . . : New York Experimentalism, 1964," Ph.D. diss., Columbia University, 2008; and Piekut, "Race, Community, and Conflict in the Jazz Composers Guild," *Jazz Perspectives* 3, no. 3 (2009): 191–231.

3. Don Heckman, "Notation and the Jazz Composer," *Down Beat*, September 23, 1965.

4. Timothy Marquand, interview with the author, March 28, 2010.

5. Robert Ostermann, "They Don't Call It Jazz: The Moody Men Who Play the New Music," *National Observer*, June 7, 1965; Ornette Coleman qtd. by Martin Williams, liner notes to *Free Jazz*, sound recording, Atlantic S-1364, 1961.

6. Dussault, "Jazznewport," *Toronto Telegram*, July 10, 1965.

7. Dan Morgenstern, "Newport Report," *Down Beat*, August 12, 1965, 24.

8. I know of no earlier available recordings that so capably spotlight her improvisations.

9. Bley qtd. in Howard Mandel, "Carla Bley: Independent Ringleader," *Down Beat*, June 1, 1978, 40.

10. Ibid.

11. Timothy Marquand, "Backgrounds," essay printed in *JCOA 1* (including Mantler's *Communications* nos. 8–11), 1968.

CHAPTER 4. "Mad at Jazz"

1. Bley qtd. in Howard Mandel, "Carla Bley: Independent Ringleader," *Down Beat*, June 1, 1978, 38.

2. Ibid.

3. Swallow, on *Marian McPartland's Piano Jazz*, radio program, NPR, recorded August 5, 1995.

4. Cream played at Fillmore Auditorium in San Francisco on August 22–27, 1967, with

the Paul Butterfield Blues Band also appearing, and again on August 29-September 2, when Gary Burton's group and the Electric Flag shared the bill.

5. The title *Silent Spring* no doubt refers to Rachel Carson's foundational environmental movement book of the same name, which had been published a few years earlier, in 1962.

6. Gary Burton, written correspondence with the author, July 2, 2009.

7. Roswell Rudd, interview with the author, November 4, 2009.

8. Bley, interview with Frank J. Oteri, "On Her Own: Carla Bley," *New Music Box*, web magazine for the American Music Center, July 1, 2003, http://www.newmusicbox.org/page .nmbx?id=51fp01.

9. Michael Mantler, written correspondence with the author, June 23, 2009.

10. Bley qtd. in Sy Johnson, "And Now, the Emerging Wacko Countess . . . Carla Bley!!!" *Jazz Magazine*, Spring 1978, 40.

CHAPTER 5. *Escalator over the Hill*

Epigraph. Roswell Rudd, interview with the author, November 4, 2009.

1. Haines's writings have been published together with writings about him; see Haines, *Secret Carnival Workers*, ed. Stuart Broomer (Toronto: Coach House, 2007).

2. Jack Cooke, "Really Beautiful," *Jazz and Blues*, June 1972.

3. In its experimental, counterculture stance, *Escalator over the Hill* bears many similarities to the Dutch opera *Reconstructie* (1969), collectively composed by Louis Andriessen, Hugo Claus, Reinbert de Leeuw, Misha Mengelberg, Harry Mulisch, Peter Schat, and Jan van Vlijmen and dedicated to Che Guevara; see Robert Adlington, "A Sort of Guerrilla: Che at the Opera," *Cambridge Opera Journal* 19, no. 2 (2007): 167–93. I am grateful to George Lewis for pointing out this connection.

4. The prepared piano was invented by John Cage around 1940. The "preparations" involve inserting various objects (usually pieces of wood and rubber or metal screws) between the strings to alter the instrument's sound.

5. See, for example, Andy Hamilton, "The Art of Improvisation and the Aesthetics of Imperfection," *British Journal of Aesthetics* 40, no. 1 (Jan. 2000): 168–85.

6. Writing along these lines, Stuart Broomer places the Bley-Haines partnership in "a sparse modern tradition of fully realized musical/verbal collaborations," including Brecht and Weill's *Threepenny Opera*, Virgil Thomson and Gertrude Stein's *Four Saints in Three Acts*, Harry Partch's *Barstow*, and Philip Glass and Robert Wilson's *Einstein on the Beach*; see Broomer, "Paul Haines: Can You Tell Me Now?" in Haines, *Secret Carnival Workers*, ed. Broomer, 219.

7. Roswell Rudd, interview with the author, November 4, 2009.

8. Michael Snow, "Paul Haines," in Haines, *Secret Carnival Workers*, ed. Broomer, 52.

9. Broomer, "Paul Haines," 217.

10. Charlie Haden, interview with the author, November 30, 2009.

11. JCOA 1 is a double album of Mantler's music recorded in May 1968, called simply *The Jazz Composer's Orchestra* and featuring as soloists Cecil Taylor, Don Cherry, Pharoah Sanders, Larry Coryell, Roswell Rudd, and Gato Barbieri. Carla Bley played piano on the recording. Timothy Marquand contributed an eloquent essay on American artistic rebels as liner notes.

12. John Fordham, "Music Reviews," *Time Out*, April 21–27, 1972; Jim Nash, "Sounds," *Penthouse*, August 1972.

CHAPTER 6. *Copyright Royalties*

1. Description printed in the NMDS twelfth-anniversary catalog in 1984.
2. Timothy Marquand, interview with the author, March 28, 2010.
3. Bley, interview with Frank J. Oteri, "On Her Own: Carla Bley," *New Music Box*, web magazine for the American Music Center, July 1, 2003, http://www.newmusicbox.org/page.nmbx?id=51fp01.
4. Zimmermann briefly spent time in the United States during 1974; he conducted the interviews for his book during 1975. Given the people with whom he had contact during that period, he was quite likely aware of the NMDS; see Walter Zimmermann, *Desert Plants: Interviews with 23 American Musicians* (Vancouver: Aesthetic Research Center Publications, 1976).
5. Bley qtd. in Howard Mandel, "Carla Bley: Independent Ringleader," *Down Beat*, January 1, 1978, 19.
6. Gregory Tate, "Forewords," *New Music Distribution Service Catalogue 1986* (New York: Jazz Composers Orchestra Association, 1986).

CHAPTER 7. *Big Band Theory*

1. Bruce qtd. in Harry Shapiro, *Jack Bruce: Composing Himself* (London: Jawbone, 2010), 189.
2. Bley, autobiographical introduction to *The Music of Carla Bley, Composed and Arranged for Piano* (Alrac Music, 1981).
3. Swallow qtd. in Barry Kernfeld, *The Story of Fake Books: Bootlegging Songs to Musicians* (Lanham, Md.: Scarecrow, 2006), 142.
4. A copy of this promotional booklet is located in the Carla Bley press clippings file at the Institute of Jazz Studies, Rutgers University, Newark, N.J.
5. Bley qtd. in Sy Johnson, "And Now, the Emerging Wacko Countess . . . Carla Bley!!!" *Jazz Magazine*, Spring 1978, 40.
6. Gary Burton, written correspondence with the author, July 2, 2009.
7. Roswell Rudd, interview with the author, November 4, 2009.
8. Bley, interview with the author, August 22, 2009. In addition, she has written of this connection in the liner notes to the composition "JonBenet," on her album *Fancy Chamber Music* (1998): "It wasn't until a week after it was finished that "JonBenet" was named. I was looking for a somewhat fragile title for this piece, which was inspired by a broken musical toy I had as a child. Then, reading a headline about the poor murdered six-year-old beauty queen, I thought, 'What an interesting name.'"
9. Bley's lyrics are "At midnight / I heard you cry / I raised my head / Got out of bed / Put on a robe / Went down the hall / Stopped at your door / For a moment / I listened there / Not a sound / I turned the knob / And entered your room / You raised your head / Got out of bed / Put on a robe / Went down the hall . . ." and so on.
10. The arrangement of *At Midnight* is strikingly similar to Robert Wyatt's "Sea Song,"

from the album *Rock Bottom*, which was produced by Nick Mason and released in 1974. I am grateful to Ma'ayan Tsadka for pointing out this connection.

11. The on-line *All Music Guide* site lists over sixty-five groups and individuals who have included her compositions on their recordings.

12. Bley qtd. in Johnson, "And Now," 43.

13. I am indebted to George Lewis for sharing his views on these matters, including comments he made during a colloquium on Bley I held at Columbia University, New York, October 23, 2009.

14. *Carla Bley: Live in Montreal*, film, dir. Pierre Lacombe, Amérimage-Spectra, 1983.

CHAPTER 8. *The Lone Arranger*

1. "Carla Bley Profiles Herself," available on-line at the official Carla Bley web site, http://www.wattxtrawatt.com (accessed Nov. 7, 2009). It is worth noting that Bley's daughter, Karen Mantler, seems to have inherited her mother's sense of irreverence; a musician, composer, and recording artist, Mantler has infamously structured much of her musical life around the topic of her cat, Arnold, who died on Mantler's birthday in 1991. Notable works in this oeuvre include the albums *My Cat Arnold* and *Karen Mantler and Her Cat Arnold Get the Flu*, and a requiem, *Arnold's Dead*. Mantler has also been an active musician in Bley's touring and recording ensembles since *Escalator over the Hill*, participating as a vocalist, keyboardist, percussionist, and harmonica player. She is also a talented visual artist and has contributed innovative and humorous cover and note design for a number of Bley's Watt recordings, as well as for the Watt Works web site.

2. Bley, unpaginated booklet accompanying *The Watt Works Family* (Munich: Watt Works/ECM, 1990).

3. Charlie Haden, telephone interview with the author, November 30, 2009.

4. Thanks to Michael Mantler for drawing my attention to Victor Borge's influence on some of Bley's musical humor.

5. Bley qtd. in Jill McManus, "Women Jazz Composers and Arrangers," *The Musical Woman* 1 (1984): 203.

6. Press release on Charlie Haden, *The Ballad of the Fallen* (arrangements by Carla Bley), sound recording, ECM 1243, 1983. Press release located in "Charlie Haden" press clippings file, Institute of Jazz Studies, Rutgers University, Newark, N.J.

7. Charlie Haden, liner notes for Liberation Music Orchestra, *Dream Keeper*, sound recording, Blue Note CDP 7 95474 2, 1990.

8. Charlie Haden, telephone interview with the author, November 30, 2009.

9. Charlie Haden, liner notes for *Liberation Music Orchestra*, sound recording, AS-9183, 1969; reissued by Impulse as IMP-11882, 1996.

10. Ibid.

11. Bley qtd. in Sy Johnson, "And Now, the Emerging Wacko Countess . . . Carla Bley!!!" *Jazz Magazine*, Spring 1978, 42.

12. The mid-nineteenth-century popular ballad tune "Annie Lisle" was "retexted" with campus-loyal lyrics first at Cornell University and the University of Kansas and later by nearly two dozen other schools.

13. Qtd. in Celeste Sunderland, "Finding Carla Bley," *All about Jazz*, June 2003, 9.

CHAPTER 9. *End of Vienna*

1. Andrzej Trzaskowski, "Record Reviews: Carla Bley—Mike Mantler," *Jazz Forum,* 1979, 38.

2. Thanks to Myra Melford for drawing this connection to my attention.

3. This description is included as "program notes" written by the composer in the CD booklet for *Fancy Chamber Music,* sound recording, Watt 28, 1998.

4. "Over There" was actually a World War I song. Bley composed another piece called *Baby Baby,* which was recorded on her first *Duets* album with Steve Swallow.

5. Bley, program note and notes to the performer, *Over There,* in *Intermediate Masterworks for Marimba,* vol. 1, ed. Nancy Zeltsman (New York: Edition Peters, 2009). During an interview, Bley described a piece she was currently working on by saying, "It's 3/4, but it's not Vienna. It's 3/4 like James Brown."

CHAPTER 10. *Dreams So Real*

1. Every musician with whom I have talked about my research for this book has unequivocally emphasized the importance of the New Music Distribution Service, especially during its early years, in the 1970s.

2. Bley qtd. in Michael Bourne, "Carla Bley and Steve Swallow: Making Sweet Music," *Down Beat,* April 1991, 19.

3. Benjamin Givan, "Thelonious Monk's Pianism," *Journal of Musicology* 26, no. 3 (Summer 2009): 429.

4. Suspension of NMDS activity had been announced in the *New York Times* as early as June 12, 1990.

5. Wilfred Dolfsma, *Institutional Economics and the Formation of Preferences: The Advent of Pop Music* (Cheltenham, U.K.: Edward Elgar, 2004), 16.

6. Bley has facetiously stated that she believes "saxophones and trumpets should consider strings as enemies, not as friends" (Bley, interview with Ben Sidran, in Sidran, *Talking Jazz: An Illustrated Oral History* [San Francisco: Pomegranate Artbooks, 1992], 181).

7. Steve Swallow, written correspondence with the author, July 6, 2009.

8. Ibid.

9. Bley, interview with Thomas Erdmann, "Writing, Creating, and the Future of Music Dissemination: An Interview with Jazz Composer and Pianist Carla Bley," *Women of Note* 8, no. 4 (2002): 8.

10. Carla Bley, interview with the author, August 22, 2009.

11. My translation; the original reads "In ihren Kompositionen und Arrangements verbindet sie teils auf groteske, teils auf ironisierende Art und Weise Elemente aus Jazz, Rock und europäischer Moderne. Hintersinnige kabarettistische und auch poetische Texte spielen eine wichtige Rolle in ihrem Schaffen. Alles zusammen verhalf ihrer Musik, angesiedelt zwischen dem Freejazz der 70er-Jahre und simplen Rocksongs, hierzulande zu einem generationenübergreifenden Publikum." The text is available at the German Jazz Trophy web site, http://www.german-jazz-trophy.de/ (accessed on Feb. 2, 2010).

12. A public interview with Bley and Swallow conducted in Stockholm in 2001 explores this topic at some length; see John Corbett, "Feeding Quarters to the Nonstop Mental Jukebox: Carla Bley and Steve Swallow in Conversation," *Down Beat,* May 2001, 36–39.

SUGGESTED LISTENING

The following chronological lists are not exhaustive; they offer selected recommendations from Carla Bley's large body of recorded work. (A comprehensive discography of Bley's recorded work up to 2004 is included as an appendix in Charles W. Turner, "I Hate to Sing: The Life and Music of Carla Bley in Her Own Words," master's thesis, Rutgers University, 2004.) The Watt Works web site (http://www.wattxtrawatt.com/) is the most complete source of information about Bley's recordings and her published, purchasable, or downloadable scores. When two years appear in parentheses, they indicate dates of recording and release, respectively. If only one appears, it is the release date.

RECORDINGS RELEASED UNDER BLEY'S NAME

Escalator over the Hill (with Paul Haines). JCOA/EOTH (1968; 1971).
Tropic Appetites. Watt 1 (1974).
13 & 3/4 (with Michael Mantler, composer of *13*). Watt 3 (1975).
Dinner Music. Watt 6 (1976; 1977).
European Tour 1977. Watt 8 (1977; 1978).
Musique Mecanique. Watt 9 (1978; 1979).
Social Studies. Watt 11 (1980; 1981).
Live! Watt 12 (1981; 1982).
I Hate to Sing. Watt 12 1/2 (1981; 1984).
Heavy Heart. Watt 14 (1983; 1984).
Night-glo. Watt 16 (1985).
Sextet. Watt 17 (1986; 1987).
Duets (with Steve Swallow). Watt 20 (1988).
Fleur Carnivore. Watt 21 (1988; 1989).
The Very Big Carla Bley Band. Watt 23 (1990; 1991).
Go Together (with Steve Swallow). Watt 24 (1992; 1993).
Big Band Theory. Watt 25 (1993).
Songs with Legs. Watt 26 (1994; 1995).

The Carla Bley Big Band Goes to Church. Watt 27 (1996).
Fancy Chamber Music. Watt 28 (1997; 1998).
Are We There Yet? (with Steve Swallow). Watt 29 (1998; 1999).
4 X 4. Watt 30 (1999; 2000).
Looking for America. Watt 31 (2002; 2003).
The Lost Chords. Watt 32 (2003; 2004).
Appearing Nightly. Watt 33 (2006; 2008).
The Lost Chords Find Paolo Fresu. Watt 34 (2007).
Carla's Christmas Carols. Watt 35 (2009).

RECORDINGS RELEASED UNDER OTHER NAMES, MUSIC COMPOSED OR ARRANGED BY BLEY

Gary Burton, *A Genuine Tong Funeral.* RCA/BMG 74321192552 (1967).
Charlie Haden, *Liberation Music Orchestra.* Impulse AS 9183 (1969).
Nick Mason, *Fictitious Sports.* SHSP 4116 (1979; 1981).
Charlie Haden, *The Ballad of the Fallen.* ECM 1248 (1983).
Charlie Haden, *Dream Keeper.* Blue Note CDP 7 95474 2 (1991).
Charlie Haden, *Not in Our Name.* Verve 80004949–02 (2005).

OTHER RECOMMENDED RECORDINGS

Paul Bley, *Solemn Meditation.* gnp31/FSR-CD 515 (1957).
George Russell Sextet, *Sextet at the Five Spot.* Decca DL 9200 (1960).
George Russell Sextet, *Stratusphunk.* Riverside RLP 9341 (1960).
George Russell Sextet, *George Russell Sextet in K.C.* Decca 74183 (1961).
Paul Bley Quintet, *Barrage.* ESP 1008 (1964).
Jazz Composer's Orchestra, *Communication.* Fontana 881 011 (1965).
Michael Mantler, *Jazz Realities.* Fontana 881 010 (1966).
Michael Mantler, *The Jazz Composer's Orchestra.* JCOA 100 1/2 (1968).
John Greaves and Peter Blegvad, *Kew. Rhone.* Voiceprint VP200CD (1976).
Gary Burton Quintet, *Dreams So Real.* ECM 1072 833 329–2 (1976).
Amarcord Nino Rota (produced by Hal Willner). Hannibal (1981).
That's the Way I Feel Now, a Tribute to Thelonious Monk. A&M CD 6600A (1984).
Lost in the Stars: The Music of Kurt Weill. A&M (1985).
Steve Swallow, *Carla.* XtraWatt 2 (1987).
For Taylor Storer. TS 001 (1988).
The Watt Works Family Album. Watt 22 (1989).
Paul Bley, *Homage to Carla.* Owl 013 427 2 (1993).

SOURCES

PRIMARY SOURCES

Press clippings and other filed materials, Institute of Jazz Studies, Rutgers University, Newark, New Jersey.

Michael Mantler, written correspondence, June 24, 2009.

Gary Burton, written correspondence, July 2 and August 25, 2009.

Steve Swallow, written correspondence, July 6 and August 26, 2009.

Carla Bley and Steve Swallow, interview, August 22, 2009.

Karen Mantler and Gary Valente, interview, September 3, 2009.

Carla Bley, telephone interview, October 1, 2009.

Roswell Rudd, interview, November 4, 2009.

Charlie Haden, telephone interview, November 30, 2009.

Timothy Marquand, interview, March 28, 2010.

SECONDARY SOURCES

Alper, Garth. "Making Sense out of Postmodern Music?" *Popular Music and Society* (2000): 1–14.

Anderson, Iain. "Jazz outside the Marketplace: Free Improvisation and Nonprofit Sponsorship of the Arts, 1965–1980." *American Music* 20, no. 2 (Summer 2002): 131–67.

———. *This Is Our Music: Free Jazz, the Sixties, and American Culture*. Philadelphia: University of Pennsylvania Press, 2007.

Bley, Carla. "Accomplishing Escalator over the Hill (1972)." In *Münchner Klavier Sommer '98; Jazz Zeitung*, June 1998.

———. "Carla Bley." Interview. *Jazz Magazine*, August 1975, 18–19.

———. "Everything Comes Together: A Conversation with Carla Bley." By Matt Weiers. *Allegro*, April 2007.

———. "Interview with Carla Bley (February 1985)." By Ben Sidran. In Sidran, *Talking Jazz: An Oral History*. San Francisco: Pomegranate Artbooks, 1992.

———. "Interview with Carla Bley: New Music's Renaissance Woman." By Titus Levi. *OPtion*, January 1985, 26–28.

————. "On Her Own: Carla Bley." Interview by Frank J. Oteri. *New Music Box*, American Music Center web magazine, July 1, 2003, http://www.newmusicbox.org/page.nmbx?id=51fp01.

————. "Writing, Creating, and the Future of Music Dissemination: An Interview with Jazz Composer and Pianist Carla Bley." By Thomas Erdmann. *Women of Note Quarterly* 8, no. 4 (2002): 3–11.

Bley, Paul. *Stopping Time: Paul Bley and the Transformation of Jazz*. Montreal: Véhicule, 1999.

Blumenthal, Bob. "Carla Bley's Avant-Garde Good Humor." *Rolling Stone*, May 3, 1979, 26, 28.

Bourne, Michael. "Carla Bley and Steve Swallow: Making Sweet Music." *Down Beat*, April 1991, 19–21.

Buhles, Günther. "Die Jazzkomponistin Carla Bley: Kurzbiographie, Werkanalyse, Würdigung" (brief biography, works analysis, assessment). *Jazzforschung* 8 (1976): 11–39.

————. "Carla Bley: Kurzbiographie, Werkanalyse, Würdigung." *Jazz Podium* 28 (January 1979): 6–11.

————. "Europa-Amerika: Die Verbindungen zwischen Neuer Musik und Jazz." *Das Orchester* 42, no. 6 (1994): 5–10.

Christgau, Robert. "New Thing." *Village Voice*, April 24, 1969.

Corbett, John. "Feeding Quarters to the Nonstop Mental Jukebox: Carla Bley and Steve Swallow." *Down Beat*, May 2001, 36–38+.

Coryell, Julie, and Laurie Friedman. *Jazz-Rock Fusion: The People, the Music*. Milwaukee, Wisc.: Hal Leonard, 1978.

Cuscuna, Mike. "Carla Bley's New Opera: Worth the Toil and Trouble." *Down Beat*, March 30, 1972.

Dahl, Linda. *Stormy Weather: The Music and Lives of a Century of Jazzwomen*. New York: Pantheon, 1984.

Daufenbach, Rolf. "Über die Männlichkeit der Musik und das Beispiel einer ungewöhnlichen Frau." *Jazz Podium* 31 (July 1982): 8–10.

Dessen, Michael. "Decolonizing Art Music: Scenes from the Late Twentieth-Century United States." Ph.D. diss., University of California, San Diego, 2003.

Dewar, Andrew Raffo. "This Is an American Music": Aesthetics, Music, and Visual Art of Bill Dixon." M.A. thesis, Wesleyan University, 2004.

Doerschuk, Robert L. "Carla Bley Actually Plays Piano on *Go Together*." *Keyboard*, June 1993, 15.

Dolfsma, Wilfred. *Institutional Economics and the Formation of Preferences: The Advent of Pop Music*. Cheltenham, U.K.: Edward Elgar, 2004.

Eckhoff, Sally. "Carla's Mood." *Village Voice*, June 20, 1995, 57, 62.

Endress, Gudrun. "Carla Bley." *Jazz Podium*, July 1989, 14–17.

————. "Escalator over the Hill." *Jazz Podium*, February 1972.

Franckling, Ken. "Carla Bley's 'Normal' Big Band." *Jazz Times*, 1992, 26–27.

Gendron, Bernard. *Between Montmartre and the Mudd Club: Popular Music and the Avant-Garde*. Chicago: University of Chicago Press, 2002.

Gioia, Ted. *West Coast Jazz: Modern Jazz in California, 1945–1960*. Berkeley: University of California Press, 1998.

Givan, Benjamin. "Thelonious Monk's Pianism." *Journal of Musicology* 26, no. 3 (Summer 2009): 404–42.

Haines, Paul. *Secret Carnival Workers*. Edited by Stuart Broomer. H. Pal Productions, 2007.

Hamilton, Andy. "The Art of Improvisation and the Aesthetics of Imperfection." *British Journal of Aesthetics* 40, no. 1 (Jan. 2000): 168–85.

Heining, Duncan. *George Russell: The Story of an American Composer*. Lanham, Md.: Scarecrow, 2010.

Heller, Michael C. " . . . So We Did It Ourselves: A Social and Musical History of Music-Organized Jazz Festivals from 1960–1973." M.A. thesis, Rutgers University, Newark, 2005.

Hinley, Patrick. "Carla Bley's Big Band." *Coda*, July–August 2003, 7–11.

Johnson, Sy. "And Now, the Emerging Wacko Countess . . . Carla Bley!!!" *Jazz Magazine*, Spring 1978, 36–43.

Jost, Ekkehard. *Jazzmusiker: Materialien zur Soziologie der afro-amerikanischen Musik*. Frankfurt: Ullstein, 1982.

Kernfeld, Barry. *The Story of Fake Books: Bootlegging Songs to Musicians*. Studies in Jazz, no. 53. Lanham, Md.: Scarecrow, 2006.

Killing, Uwe. "Carla Bley—Steve Swallow." *Jazz Podium*, April 1988, 33.

Kozinn, Allan. "New Music Record Distributor Is Closing." *New York Times*, June 12, 1990.

Lachner, Harry. "Carla Bley: Alles paßt." *Süddeutsche Zeitung*, July 13, 1998.

Levin, Robert. "The Jazz Composers Guild: An Assertion of Dignity." *Down Beat*, May 6, 1965, 17–18.

Lewis, George E. "Experimental Music in Black and White: The AACM in New York, 1970—1985." In *Uptown Conversation*, edited by Robert G. O'Meally, Brent Hayes Edwards, and Farah Jasmine Griffin (New York: Columbia University Press, 2004), 75–79.

Lewis, George E. *A Power Stronger Than Itself: The AACM and American Experimental Music*. Chicago: University of Chicago Press, 2008.

Linke, Hans Jürgen. "Humor und Virtuosität: Die Big Carla Bley Band." *Neue Musikzeitung*, April–May 1989, 14.

Macnie, Jim. "Carla Bley's Career Has Legs." *Billboard*, June 29, 1996, 1–2.

Magee, Jeffrey. *The Uncrowned King of Swing: Fletcher Henderson and Big Band Jazz*. New York: Oxford University Press, 2005.

Mandel, Howard. "Carla Bley: Independent Ringleader." *Down Beat*, June 1, 1978, 18–19+.

———. *Future Jazz*. New York: Oxford University Press, 1999.

———. "The Hymn of the Hopeful." *Village Voice*, December 20, 1983, 101–2.

McManus, Jill. "Women Jazz Composers and Arrangers." *The Musical Woman* 1 (1983–84): 197–208.

O'Brien, Karen. *Hymn to Her: Women Musicians Talk*. London: Virago, 1995.

Page, Tim. "They Sell the Small Record Labels." *New York Times*, March 14, 1983.

Palmer, Don. "My Dinner With Carla." *Down Beat*, August 1984, 24–26.

Parales, Jon. "Carla Bley's Playground." *Village Voice*, May 22, 1978, 56, 58.

Piekut, Benjamin D. "Race, Community, and Conflict in the Jazz Composers Guild." *Jazz Perspectives* 3, no. 3 (2009): 191–231.

———. "The Jazz Composers Guild and Black Experimentalism." Chapter 2 of "Testing, Testing. . . . : New York Experimentalism, 1964." Ph.D. diss., Columbia University, 2008.

———. "New Thing? Gender and Sexuality in the Jazz Composers Guild." *American Quarterly* 62, no. 1 (2010): 25–48.

Porter, Lewis. "You Can't Get Up There Timidly." *Music Educators Journal* 71 (Oct. 1984): 42–46.

Price, Emmett George III. "Free Jazz and the Black Arts Movement, 1958–1967." Ph.D. diss., University of Pittsburgh, 2000.

Quénum, Thierry. "Carla Bley and Paul Haines." *Jazz Magazine*, October 1998, 8–9.

Rudd, Roswell. "Interview with Roswell Rudd." By David Dupont. *Cadence*, November 1992, 8–19.

Saul, Scott. *Freedom Is, Freedom Ain't: Jazz and the Making of the Sixties*. Cambridge, Mass.: Harvard University Press, 2003.

Schneider, Rolf D. "Die Musik von Carla Bley und Michael Mantler." *Jazz Podium*, November 1980, 10–11.

Shapiro, Harry. *Jack Bruce: Composing Himself*. London: Jawbone, 2010.

Shoemaker, Bill. "Big Bands, Orchestral Visions." *Jazz Times*, Jan.–Feb. 1992, 28–30.

Smith, Arnold Jay, and Bob Henschen. "Electronic Projections." *Down Beat*, January 13, 1977, 16–17.

Sweet, Robert E. *Music Universe, Music Mind: Revisiting the Creative Music Studio, Woodstock, New York*. Ann Arbor, Mich.: Arborville, 1996.

Trzaskowski, Andrzej. "Record Reviews: Carla Bley—Mike Mantler." *Jazz Forum*, 1979 37–40.

Taylor, Jeffrey. "Carla Bley Biography." *Contemporary Musicians*. Vol. 8. Farmington Hills, Mich.: Gale Research, 1992.

Tucker, Sherrie. "Bordering on Community: Improvising Women Improvising Women-in-Jazz." In *The Other Side of Nowhere: Jazz, Improvisation, and Communities in Dialogue*. Edited by Daniel Fischlin and Ajay Heble (Middletown, Conn.: Wesleyan University Press, 2004), 244–67.

Turner, Charles W. "I Hate to Sing: The Life and Music of Carla Bley in Her Own Words." M.A. thesis, Rutgers University, 2004.

"Under the Volcano: A Conversation with Carla Bley, Steve Swallow, Mike Mantler, and Jack Cumming." *Coda*, February–March 1987: 4–5.

Williams, Martin. *Jazz Changes*. New York: Oxford University Press, 1992.

Wilson, Peter Niklas. *Hear and Now: Gedanken zur improvisierten Musik*. Hofheim, Germany: Wolke, 1999.

Zabor, Rafi. "Carla Bley, The Toast of the Continent: America's Great and Neglected Post-Bop, Pre-Avant, Neo-Modern Fe-male Jazz Composer." *Musician, Player, and Listener*, August 1981, 64–70.

INDEX

13 (Michael Mantler), 56

Abbey Road (The Beatles), 87
Abrams, Muhal Richard, 54, 63
Adagio for Strings (Barber), 81
Adams, Terry, 69
African National Congress anthem, 71
Alrac Music, 31, 76
"Amazing Grace," 69
"America the Beautiful," 69, 74
Anderson, Arlene (Bley's mother), 6
Anderson, Laurie, 53
Apfelbaum, Peter, 63
Apollonian personality, 18
Archie Shepp Quartet, 28
Archie Shepp Trio, 31
Art Ensemble of Chicago, 30, 45
Ashley, Robert, 45, 52, 83
Association for the Advancement of Cre-
    ative Musicians (AACM), 28, 60
"As You Said" (Cream), 49
Atlantic Records, 12, 52
Avignon festival, 89
Ayler, Albert, 27, 30, 37, 45

Bailey, Derek, 46
Baker, Chet, 7
Balanescu, Alexander, 87
Balanescu Quartet, 87
Ballad of the Fallen (Liberation Music
    Orchestra), 66
Barber, Samuel, 69, 81
Barbieri, Gato, 3, 36, 38, 43, 44, 48, 71, 94

Barcelona (Spain), 58
Bard College, 11
Barrage (Paul Bley), 14, 30
Bartók, Béla, 88
Basie, Count, 8, 31, 88, 89
Basin Street, 8, 12
Bear Comes Home, The (Rafi Zabor), 1
Beatles, The, 34, 40, 46, 50, 66, 87, 88, 89
Beethoven, Ludwig van, 5, 25, 66, 73, 89
Berger, Karl, 43, 63
Berkeley (Calif.), 6
Berklee College of Music, 32, 58
Berlin Jazz Festival, 87
Bill Dixon Sextet, 28
Birdland, 1, 3, 8, 90
Bitches Brew (Davis), 50
Black Artists' Group (St. Louis), 28
Black Hawk, The, 7
Black Orchid, The, 7, 90
Black Saint, 53
Blake, Ran, 11
Blakey, Art, 31
Bleecker Street, 10, 12
Blegvad, Peter, 57
Bley, Carla: *3/4*, 55–56, 65, 75–76, 80;
    440, 61, 65; *4x4*, 65, 87; *Adagio for
    Strings* (Barber), 81; *Ad Infinitum*, 18,
    65; *America the Beautiful*, 74; "Anthem,"
    73; *Appearing Nightly at the Black
    Orchid*, 90; *Are We There Yet?* (with
    Swallow), 16, 62, 84; *Around Again*,
    18, 25; as arranger, 69–74; *At Mid-
    night (Musique Mecanique pt. 2)*, 62;

The Banana Quintet, 65, 87; *Bars*, 59; *Batterie*, 17, 18; *Beast Blues*, 14; *Bent Eagle*, 14, 65; *Big Band Theory*, 87; *Birds of Paradise*, 87; and blues, 16; *Blues in Twelve Bars and Blues in Twelve Other Bars*, 65; *Blunt Object*, 65; *Boo to You Too*, 65; "Business Men," 46; Carla Bley Band, 26; *The Carla Bley Big Band Goes to Church*, 81, 87; *Carla's Christmas Carols*, 26, 89; and church music, 5, 6, 85, 87–88; *Closer*, 21, 22, 24; *Coppertone*, 76; cowboy song, 6; *Dance Class*, 14; *Death Rolls*, 38; *Detective Writer Daughter*, 41; *Dinner Music*, 25, 53; dirge, 6; *Doctor*, 32; *Donkey*, 9, 14, 16; *Dreams So Real* (Burton), 56; *Drinking Music*, 62; *Duets* (with Swallow), 78, 84, 85; *Early Short Pieces*, 15–26; *Emphasis*, 14; *End of Vienna*, 80, 81; *Escalator Over the Hill*, 2, 14, 26, 40, 41–50, 51, 52, 53, 58, 61, 70, 80, 82, 89, 90; *Essence*, 14; *European Tour 1977*, 60, 61, 62; *Exaltation* (Ruggles), 81, 87; *Fancy Chamber Music*, 62, 75–82, 86; *Fanfare*, 38; *Fast Lane*, 61; *Fictitious Sports* (with Mason), 63, 64, 69; *Flags*, 24–25, 60, 73; *Fleur Carnivore*, 65, 86; Floater, 18–19, 78; *The Funnybird Song*, 53; *Generous 1*, 22, 24; *A Genuine Tong Funeral*, 35–40, 42, 49, 60, 80; *The Girl Who Cried Champagne*, 65; "God Mother," 74; *Go Together* (with Swallow), 84; "Grand Mother," 74; *Grave Train*, 36, 38–39; *Healing Power*, 87; *Heavy Heart*, 60, 85; High Mass for Low Brass, 65; *Hip Hop*, 65; "Holiday in Risk Theme," 47; *Holy Roller Coaster*, 89; "Hotel Lobby Band," 47; and humor, 61, 62, 65–69, 71; *Ictus*, 14, 16–18, 25; *Ida Lupino*, 18, 25, 65, 66; *I Hate to Sing*, 45, 60, 67–68, 84; *I'm a Mineralist*, 69; and "imperfection," 44–45, 61, 78; *Intermission Music*, 37, 38, 65, 78, 80; *In the Morning Out There*, 14; *It's Rotten*, 64; *Jesus Maria*, 14, 26, 33, 48, 62; *Jesus Maria and Other Spanish Strains*, 61–62; "Keep it Spangled," 73; *King Korn*, 16, 18, 60, 73; *Lawns*, 65; *Live!*, 60, 65, 87; *Liver of Life*, 65; *The Lone Arranger*, 64; *Looking for America*, 73–74; *The Lord is Listening To Ya, Hallelujah!*, 64, 86, 87; The Lost Chords, 87; march, 6; and "mistakes," 7, 62; *More Brahms*, 65, 81; *Morning (pt. 1 and 2)*, 36, 38; *Mother of the Dead Man*, 36, 38; *Musique Mecanique*, 26, 45, 60, 61–62, 84; *My Father's Record*, 87–88; *The New Funeral March*, 36, 38; *A New Hymn*, 18, 87; *The New National Anthem*, 36, 39, 60, 73, 74; *Night-glo*, 66, 85; *And Now, the Queen*, 22–24, 25, 60, 65, 73, 78; "OG Can UC?," 73; "O Holy Night," 89–90; *Oni Puladi*, 18, 32–33; *On the Stage in Cages*, 65; *The Opening*, 38, 39; opera, 6, 36; *O Plus One*, 9; *Over the Hill*, 6, 41; *Over There*, 80, 81–82; *Overtoned*, 65; *Paws without Claws*, 65; Penny Cillin, 63; as performer, 32–33, 43–44, 57–58, 64, 82, 84–86; *Piano Lesson*, 68; and political themes, 66, 69–74; polka, 6; and "punk jazz," 63–64, 69; and quotation, 66, 69; *Rawalpindi Blues*, 26, 46, 48, 49; *Reactionary Tango*, 65; *Roast*, 29, 37; *Romantic Notions*, 21, 76–80, 84; *Setting Calvin's Waltz*, 65, 87; *Sextet*, 84; *Sex with Birds*, 65, 66; *Shovels*, 38, 39; *Silent Spring*, 36, 38; *Sing Me Softly of the Blues*, 16, 65; *Social Studies*, 60; *Some Dirge*, 36, 38; *Someone to Watch*, 66; songs, 6; *Song Sung Long*, 65; *Songs with Legs*, 86; *Songs Without Words*, 18, 25, 79; "Soon I Will Be Done with the Troubles of the World," 85, 87; *Spangled Banner Minor*, 25, 60, 65, 73, 74; "Step Mother," 74; *Strange Arrangement*, 65; *The Survivors*, 36, 39; *Syndrome*, 18, 25; *Thesis*, 14; *Tigers in Training*, 62; *Tijuana Traffic*, 61; *Tropical Appetites*, 53; *United States*, 74, 86; *Ups and Downs*, 64, 66–67; *Utviklingssang*, 65, 66, 85; *Valse Sinistre*, 65, 80, 81; Variations on "Onward Christian Soldier," 6; *Vashkar*, 18, 26, 48; *The Very Big Carla Bley Band*, 74; *Very, Very Sim-*

ple, 68; *Violin*, 21–22, 24; *Vox Humana*, 18; *Walking Batterie Woman*, 17–18, 64; *Walking Woman*, 2, 18, 19–21, 30, 78; waltz, 6, 37, 55, 75–76, 80, 81; "Whose Broad Stripes," 73; *Who Will Rescue You?*, 87; "Why," 47; *Wildlife*, 66; *Wolfgang Tango*, 80, 81; *Wrong Key Donkey*, 65; "Your Mother," 74

Bley, Paul, 3, 8–16, 18, 25, 28–31, 45, 46

Blue Note Records, 52

BMG-Bertelsmann Records, 86

BMI, 89

Borg, Carla (Carla Bley), 9

Borg, Emil Carl (Bley's father), 5, 9, 15, 87–88

Borg, Karen (Carla Bley), 9

Borg, Lovella May (Carla Bley), 5, 90

Borge, Victor, 68

Bottom Line, 60

Brahms, Johannes, 80, 81, 88

Braxton, Anthony, 52, 63

Brecht, Berthold, 39

Broomer, Stuart, 46

Brötzmann, Peter, 34, 39

Brown, Earle, 29, 59

Brubeck, Dave, 7, 28

Bruce, Jack, 3, 35, 43, 44, 46, 48, 49, 57–59, 63

"Bulldog Up at Yale Has No Tail, The," 7

Burma Club, 7

Burning Sensations, 63

Burton, Gary, 3, 12, 35–38, 56, 60

Bush, George W., 72, 74

Byron, Michael, 54

Café Bohemia, 8, 10

Cage, John, 29, 52, 55, 63, 69, 83, 94

Cambridge University (England), 58

Carla (Swallow), 84

Carla Bley Band, The, 59–64, 65, 86

Carter, Kent, 32

Castlemont High School (Oakland), 6

Cecil Taylor Unit, 28

Cellar, The (Vancouver), 9

Cellar Café, 28

Chadbourne, Eugene, 61

Chambers Street, 28

Chatham, Rhys, 52

Chatham Square (record label), 53, 54

Cherry, Don, 3, 9, 30, 43, 44, 48, 53, 94

Choice Records, 54

Chopin, Frédéric, 5, 66

chronotransduction, 42, 48, 49

church music, 5, 70

Cinematheque, 44

Circle-in-the-Square Theater, 11

Circus '68 '69 (Haden), 72

Civilization Phaze III (Zappa), 49

Clark, John, 60

Cohen, Paul, 11

Coleman, Ornette, 9–12, 22, 27, 28, 30, 31, 32, 33, 40, 42, 55, 69, 71, 74

Coleman Classics Vol. 1, 9

College of William and Mary (Virginia), 86

Coltrane, John, 8, 10, 11, 27, 31

Columbia Records, 50, 52

Communication (JCO; Fontana Records), 29, 45

Concept (record label), 54

concept album, 34–35, 40

Conjure (Hanrahan), 64

Contemporary Center (Seventh Avenue), 29

Corea, Chick, 53, 56

Coryell, Larry, 35, 38, 94

Count Basie Orchestra, The, 31

Cowell, Henry, 3, 52, 54, 59

Cream, 35, 49, 93–94

Creative Music Studio (Woodstock, N.Y.), 63

CRI, 53, 54

"Crown Him with Many Crowns," 88

Davidson, Lowell, 32

Davies, Dennis Russell, 3, 56

Davis, Miles, 8, 10, 11, 26, 31, 50

"Day in the Life, A" (The Beatles), 34, 40

Dear C.: The Music of Carla Bley, 89

Debussy, Claude, 22, 70

Democratic National Convention (Chicago 1968), 72

Desert Plants (Zimmermann), 55

Desto Records, 54

"Deutschland Über Alles," 60, 73
Dionysian personality, 18
Dixon, Bill, 13, 27, 28–29, 33
Dolfsma, Wilfred, 8
Dolphy, Eric, 12, 13
Down Beat, 7, 29, 33, 35, 42, 52, 91
Dream Keeper (Liberation Music Orchestra), 66, 69, 70
Dreams So Real (Burton), 56
Drummond, Billy, 87
Dvořák, Antonin, 39, 69, 81
Dylan, Bob, 31

ECM Records, 3, 53, 54, 56, 68, 76, 86
Eicher, Manfred, 53
Einstein on the Beach (Glass), 69, 94
Eisler, Hanns, 69
Electric Circus (New York), 42
Ellington, Edward Kennedy ("Duke"), 28, 37, 60, 61, 63, 70, 86, 88
Ellis, Don, 12, 13, 14
"El Pueblo Unido Jamás Será Vencido," 69
"El Quinto Regimento" (Liberation Music Orchestra), 71
EMI Records, 86
Eno, Brian, 63
Ensemble, The, 55, 75–76
Ertegun, Nesuhi, 52
ESP-Disk records, 30–31
Evers, Medgar, 70
Exaltation (Ruggles), 81, 87
Ezz-thetics (Russell), 12

Fabulous Paul Bley Quintet, The, 9
Farmer, Art, 3, 12
Feather, Leonard, 31
Feinberg, Alan, 76
Feldman, Morton, 78
Fictitious Sports (Mason/Bley), 63, 64
Fillmore, The, 35
Finnadar (record label), 54
Fitzgerald, Ella, 91
Five Spot, The, 10, 11, 27, 29
"Flamenco Sketches," 26
"Flying Home Band, The," 7
Folwell, Bill, 13

Footloose (Paul Bley), 45
Ford Foundation, 51
"Forever and Sunsmell" (Cage), 63
Fort Ord, 7
found sound, 71
Four Days in December (1964), 28, 29
"Fourth of July" (Ives), 73
Free Form Improvisation Ensemble, 28
free jazz, 9, 11–12, 22, 25, 30, 34, 37, 39, 64, 71
Free Jazz (Coleman), 11–12
Free Music Production, 53
Fresu, Paolo, 87
Frick Middle School (Oakland), 6
Frisell, Bill, 69
Frith, Fred, 52, 83
fusion, 49, 50

Gamelan Son of Lion, 83
Garland, Peter, 54
Gary, Bruce, 57
Gary Burton Quartet, 36
Gaye, Marvin, 88
Gebhardt, Steve, 43
German Jazz Trophy, 90
Gershwin, George, 16, 66
Getz, Stan, 8, 31
Giant Steps (Coltrane), 11
Gillespie, Dizzy, 8, 28, 66
Giuffre, Jimmy, 3, 10, 12, 13, 26
Givan, Benjamin, 86
Glasgow Jazz Festival, 87
Glass, Philip, 53, 69
"God Save the Queen," 73
Goodrich, Mick, 56
Gordon, David, 12
Gordon, Max, 35
Graham, Martha, 33
Grand Central Station, 8
Grand Prix du Disque du Jazz (France, 1973), 52
Graz (Austria), 14
Greaves, John, 57
Greene, Burton, 29
Greenwich Village (New York City), 10, 11, 12, 13, 42
Grieg, Edvard, 6

Grog Kill Studio, 57, 86
Guggenheim grant, 50

Haden, Charlie, 2, 3, 9–10, 22, 39, 41, 42,
    43, 44, 47, 49, 61, 66, 69–72
Haines, Jo Hayward, 27
Haines, Paul, 27, 30, 41–43, 45–48, 53, 90
Half Note, The, 29
Hall, Ray, 42, 49
Hampton, Lionel, 7
Handel, Georg Friedrich, 87
Hanrahan, Kip, 64
"Happy Days are Here Again," 72
Haring, Keith, 56
Harrison, Lou, 52
Harvard University, 30
Havenscourt Colonial Church (Oakland,
    Calif.), 5
Hawkins, Coleman, 29
Heckman, Don, 29
Henderson, Fletcher, 28
Hentoff, Nat, 70, 83–84
Heron, Gil-Scott, 53, 56
Higgins, Billy, 9
Hillcrest Club, The (Los Angeles), 3,
    9–10
Hines, Earl, 31
Holiday, Billy, 91
Hughes, Langston, 69
hungry i, The, 7
Hurrah's, 64

Impetus magazine, 42
impressionism, 22
In C (Riley), 25
International Critics Poll award (Down
    Beat), 33, 42
"I've Got Rhythm" (Gershwin), 16
Ives, Charles, 5, 33, 70, 73
Ivy League songs, 7
"I Want You (She's so Heavy)" (The
    Beatles), 87

Jack Bruce Band, 57–59
Jarrett, Keith, 3, 56, 76
Jazz Composers Guild, 3, 28–32, 33, 51
Jazz Composers Guild Orchestra, 28, 29

Jazz Composers Orchestra (JCO), 31, 33,
    42, 44, 45, 51, 54, 56
Jazz Composers Orchestra Association
    (JCOA), 28, 33, 49, 51, 52, 53
Jazz Gallery, The, 12
"Jazzman of the Year" (1968), 35
jazz opera, 2, 41–50
Jazz Realities (group) and Jazz Realities
    (recording), 32–33
Jazz Record Center, 28
JCOA, 1, 94
"Jeepers Creepers," 89
Jenkins, Leroy, 43, 44
Jimmy Giuffre Trio, 13
Johnson, Howard, 36, 69
Jones, Paul, 43
Jones, Philly Joe, 10
Joplin, Scott, 63
Jordan, Sheila, 43
Judson Hall, 28

Kaiser, Henry, 52
Kew. Rhone. (Greaves and Blegvad), 57
Kind of Blue (Davis), 11
King, Martin Luther, 70
Knepper, Jimmy, 36, 38
Kowald, Peter, 34, 39

Lacy, Steve, 10, 13, 32, 36, 38
LaFaro, Scott, 9
Leahy, Ronnie, 57
Lee, Jeanne, 43
Le Figaro (New York), 13
Lenox School of Jazz (Massachusetts),
    10, 12
Lentz, Daniel, 52
"Let the Lower Light Be Burning," 88
Lewis, George, 60, 63, 96
Liberation Music Orchestra, 3, 10, 39, 41,
    42, 51, 66, 69–74, 81. See also Haden,
    Charlie
"Lift Every Voice and Sing," 69, 74
Lincoln Center (New York), 55, 76, 89
Lindsay, Arto, 83
"Little Help from My Friends, A" (The
    Beatles), 40
Los Angeles, 3, 9–10, 16

"Los Quatros Generales" (Liberation Music Orchestra), 71
Lovano, Joe, 64
Lowry, Malcolm, 63
Lucier, Alvin, 52
"Lucy in the Sky with Diamonds" (The Beatles), 46
Ludwigsburg (Germany), 86
Luescher, Fredi, 89
Lydian Chromatic Concept of Tonal Organization, The (Russell), 11, 12

MacDougal Street's Playhouse, 13
Macero, Teo, 8, 52, 88
Malcolm X, 70
Mannes School of Music, 30
Mantler, Karen, 33, 43, 45, 53, 61, 84, 87, 88, 91, 96
Mantler, Michael, 3, 28–33, 35, 36, 38, 41, 43, 44, 50–53, 56, 58–59, 69, 80, 83, 86, 94
Mark, Ilene, 76
Marquand, Timothy, 27, 29, 33, 43, 52, 54, 76, 94
Marsalis, Wynton, 89
"Marseillaise," 73
Marsh, Warne, 46
Mason, Nick, 63, 64, 69, 96
McBrown, Lennie, 9
McLaughlin, John, 3, 43, 48
McPartland, Marian, 7, 77, 92
McRae, Carmen, 31
Mekas, Jonas, 44
Melody Maker (England), 52
Melville, Herman, 33
Mendelssohn, Felix, 18
Messiah, The (Handel), 87
Metheny, Pat, 56, 69
Milhaud, Darius, 22, 70
Miller, Claude, 60
Mingus, Charles, 3, 8, 10, 27, 28, 29, 37, 61, 70, 83
minimalism, 69
Mixed Bag (WGBH-Boston), 35
Mobil Foundation, 51
modal jazz, 24
Moffett, Charles, 13

Moncur, Grachan, III, 53
Monk, Thelonious, 8, 12, 13, 18, 22, 31, 32, 64, 78, 86, 88
Monterey Jazz Festival, 90
Morgenstern, Dan, 31
Morris, Butch, 83
Mortelle Randonee (film), 60
Moses, Bob, 35, 56
Mothers of Invention, 53
Motian, Paul, 3, 43, 44
Mourir à Madrid (film), 71
Mulligan, Gerry, 7
Mumma, Gordon, 52
Murray, Sonny, 27, 30
Musée Mécanique (San Francisco), 61
Musica Elettronica Viva, 45
Music in Fifths (Glass), 53
Music in Similar Motion (Glass), 53
Music with Changing Parts (Glass), 53
"My Country 'Tis of Thee," 73

National Endowment for the Arts, 30, 51
National Public Radio, 72
"Nearer My God to Thee," 5
New Christie Minstrels, 7
New England Holidays (Ives), 73
Newman, Randy, 43
New Music (Cowell), 3
New Music America, 63
New Music Distribution Service (NMDS), 3, 51–56, 67, 83–84, 86
Newport Jazz Festival (1965), 3, 31
New World Symphony (Dvorák), 39, 81
New York Art Quartet, 28, 30, 45
New York Eye and Ear Control (Snow/ Ayler), 30, 45
New York Herald Tribune, 31
New York State Council for the Arts, 51
New York Times, 27, 54, 72
"Ninety and Nine, The," 88
Norddeutscher Rundfunk, 80, 86
Not in Our Name (Liberation Music Orchestra), 39, 66, 74, 81

Oakland Youth Chorus, 70
Oblivion (record label), 54
Obscure (record label), 63

October Revolution in Jazz (1964), 3, 28, 30, 32, 52
O'Day, Anita, 8
"Old MacDonald Had a Farm," 74
Oliveros, Pauline, 52
Olshausen, Cécile, 89
Omaha World Herald, 50
ONCE Festival, 60
Ono, Yoko, 42
"Onward Christian Soldier," 6, 80
Oppens, Ursula, 3, 56, 76
Opus One, 53, 54
Originale (Stockhausen), 13–14, 43
"Over There," 81

Papp, Joseph, 33, 42, 83
Parade (Satie), 5
Parker, Charlie, 8, 33
Partch, Harry, 45, 49, 52, 83, 84
Paul Bley Quartet, 31
Paul Bley Quintet, 28
Peacock, Annette, 27
Peacock, Gary, 27, 30, 31
Penthouse, 50
Penthouse/Windsor Steak House (Montreal), 9
People's Music Works, 54
Phase 2, 12–13
Pike, Dave, 9
Pink Floyd, 63
Polansky, Larry, 54
Pollock, Jackson, 12, 33
Pop, Iggy, 60
Portsmouth Sinfonia, The, 45
Powell, Bud, 8
"Power in the Blood of the Lamb," 5
Preston, Don, 43, 53
Public Theater, 33, 42, 83
Purple Onion, The, 7
Puschnig, Wolfgang, 62, 76

Rachmaninov, Sergei, 6
Ravel, Maurice, 22, 70, 76
RCA, 35, 42
Real Book, The, 58, 84
Reconstructie, 94
Redman, Dewey, 3, 71

Reed, Ishmael, 64
Return to Forever (Corea), 56
Riley, Terry, 25
Roach, Max, 28
Robinson, Perry, 43
Rock Bottom (Wyatt), 69
"Rock of Ages," 5
roller skating, 6
Rolling Stones, The, 57
Rollins, Sonny, 16
Romano, Also, 32
Ronstadt, Linda, 43, 47, 49
Roswell Rudd-John Tchicai Quartet, 28
Rudd, Roswell, 3, 10, 12, 13, 27–30, 37, 41, 43–46, 48, 60, 62, 71, 72, 74, 94
Ruggles, Carl, 81, 87
Russell, George, 3, 10, 11, 12, 14, 24
Rzewski, Frederic, 55, 63

Sabino, Peter, 28
"Salt Peanuts" (Gillespie), 66
Sam Goody shops, 28
Sanders, Pharoah, 94
San Francisco Bay Area, 7, 35, 67
Saunders, Ted, 64
Sausalito (California), 35
Satie, Erik, 5, 18, 22, 69, 70, 93
Schoenberg, Arnold, 45
Scratch Orchestra, The, 45
Seeger, Pete, 31
Sgt. Pepper's Lonely Hearts Club Band (The Beatles), 34, 40, 50
Shannon, Robert, 76
Shape of Jazz to Come, The (Coleman), 10–11
Sharpe, D., 45, 67, 69
Shepp, Archie, 12, 28, 29, 31
Sheppard, Andy, 62, 87
Shostakovich, Dmitri, 37, 80, 89
Sidran, Ben, 48
signifying, 6
Silver, Horace, 29
Sinatra, Frank, 31
Skies of America (Coleman), 74
Slagle, Steve, 64
Smith, Bessie, 91
Snow, Michael, 30, 34, 44, 45

Soft Machine, 69
Solemn Meditation (Paul Bley), 9
Soloff, Lew, 62
"Someone to Watch over Me" (Gershwin), 66
Something Else! (Coleman), 9
Song for Che (Haden), 71
Sony Records, 86
Sousa, John Philip, 73
Sparks, Randy, 7
Speculum Musicae, 56
Speeth, Sheridan ("Sherry"), 42
Spiritual Unity (Ayler), 45
"Stars and Stripes Forever" (Sousa), 73
"Star Spangled Banner," 24, 73, 86
Stephen, Edith, 29
Stewart, Bob, 53
Stockhausen, Karlheinz, 13, 43
Stollman, Bernard, 31
Storer, Taylor, 54, 67
Stratusphunk (Russell), 14
Stravinsky, Igor, 18, 81, 88
Su, Nathanael, 89
Summer of Love, 34
Sun Ra, 28, 29
Supremes, The, 81, 88
Survival (record label), 54
Swallow, Steve, 2, 3, 11–13, 15, 22, 27, 35, 36, 56, 58, 62, 63, 66, 68, 69, 78, 84–89
Sweet Basil, 12
Symphony of Psalms (Stravinsky), 81

"Take the "A" Train" (Ellington), 61
Take Three Coffee House, 13
Tate, Gregory, 52, 56
Taylor, Cecil, 13, 27, 28, 29, 31, 32, 33, 52, 92, 94
Taylor, Mick, 57
Tchicai, John, 28, 29, 30, 46
Third Stream, 2, 49, 55
Thornton, Clifford, 53
Threadgill, Henry, 52, 83
Threepenny Opera (Weill/Brecht), 39, 94
Tin Pan Alley songs, 7, 11–12
Tomorrow Is the Question! (Coleman), 9
Toronto Telegram, 31
Townshend, Pete, 42

Tribe Records, 54
Trident, The, 35
Tristano, Lennie, 27
Turning Point (Paul Bley), 25
Tyranny, "Blue" Gene, 60

Under the Volcano (Lowry), 63
Universal Records, 86

Valente, Gary, 62, 69
Varèse, Edgard, 52
Vaughan, Sarah, 91
Velvet Underground, 42
Very Big Carla Bley Band, The, 86
Vienna (Austria), 31, 32, 80, 81
Village Vanguard, The, 29, 35, 45
Virgin Records, 52, 57
Viva, 43, 45
"Viva La Quince Brigada" (Liberation Music Orchestra), 71

Warhol, Andy, 42
Warner/Time Warner Records, 86
War Orphans (Coleman), 71
Watt Family Scrapbook (1994), 54
Watt Works (record label), 52, 53, 55, 58–59, 68, 76, 86
Watt Works Family (1990), 54, 68
WCKR (Columbia University), 67
Wealth of Carols, A, 33
Webern, Anton von, 20, 88, 89
Weill, Kurt, 39, 58, 64, 88, 89
"We Shall Overcome," 69, 72
Westdeutscher Rundfunk, 63
"What a Friend We Have in Jesus," 88
What's New? (Macero), 8
"Where Did Our Love Go?" (The Supremes), 81
"Whiffenpoof Song, The," 7
White Light (Pollock), 12
Wilkins, Ernie, 88
Williams, Mary Lou, 91
Williams, Tony, 3
Willner, Hal, 64
Willow (NY), 1, 57, 89
Windo, Gary, 69
Winter, John, 29

Winter in America (Heron), 56
Wolff, Christian, 29, 63
Wolff, Francis, 52
"Wonderful Widow of Eighteen Springs, The" (Cage), 63
Woodstock Creative Music Foundation, 63
Wuorinen, Charles, 88, 89
Wyatt, Robert, 63, 69, 95–96

XtraWatt, 84

Yale University, 10, 11, 12, 13
"Yankee Doodle," 73
Young, Lester, 8
"You're a Grand Old Flag," 72
Ypsilanti (Michigan), 59

Zabor, Rafi (*The Bear Comes Home*), 1
Zappa, Frank, 49
Zimmermann, Walter, 55
Zorn, John, 53, 54, 83

AMERICAN

Composers

Lou Harrison
  Leta E. Miller and Fredric Lieberman

John Cage
  David Nicholls

Dudley Buck
  N. Lee Orr

William Grant Still
  Catherine Parsons Smith

Rudolf Friml
  William Everett

Elliott Carter
  James Wierzbicki

Carla Bley
  Amy C. Beal

AMY C. BEAL is a professor of music at the University of California, Santa Cruz, and the author of *New Music, New Allies: American Experimental Music in West Germany from the Zero Hour to Reunification*.

The University of Illinois Press
is a founding member of the
Association of American University Presses.

University of Illinois Press
1325 South Oak Street
Champaign, IL 61820-6903
www.press.uillinois.edu